Powerful Products

Powerful Products

Strategic Management of Successful New Product Development

Roger Bean
Russell Radford

American Management Association

New York • Atlanta • Boston • Chicago • Kansas City • San Francisco • Washington, D. C.
Brussels • Mexico City • Tokyo • Toronto

Special discounts on bulk quantities of AMACOM books are available to corporations, professional associations, and other organizations. For details, contact Special Sales Department, AMACOM, a division of American Management Association, 1601 Broadway, New York, NY 10019.
Tel.: 212-903-8316. Fax: 212-903-8083.
Web site: www.amanet.org

This publication is designed to provide accurate and authoritative information in regard to the subject matter covered. It is sold with the understanding that the publisher is not engaged in rendering legal, accounting, or other professional service. If legal advice or other expert assistance is required, the services of a competent professional person should be sought.

Library of Congress Cataloging-in-Publication Data

Bean, Roger
 Powerful products: strategic management of successful new product development / Roger Bean, Russell Radford.
   p. cm.
 Includes bibliographical references and index.
 ISBN 0-8144-0566-5
 1. Product management. 2. New products—Marketing. I. Radford, Russell W. II. Title.
 HF5415.15.B38 2000
 658.5'75—dc21   00–024828

© 2000 Roger Bean and Russell Radford.
All rights reserved.
Printed in the United States of America.

This publication may not be reproduced,
stored in a retrieval system,
or transmitted in whole or in part,
in any form or by any means, electronic,
mechanical, photocopying, recording, or otherwise,
without the prior written permission of AMACOM,
a division of American Management Association,
1601 Broadway, New York, NY 10019.

Printing number

10 9 8 7 6 5 4 3 2 1

Contents

	Preface	vii
	Acknowledgments	xi
1.	Strategic Product Development	1
2.	The Genesis of New Products	19
3.	Strategic Opportunities and Responsibilities	33
4.	A Strategic Understanding of Customer Needs	51
5.	Product Development and Corporate Culture	69
6.	The New Product Decision Screen	85
7.	Staffing the Development Activity	97
8.	Managing Existing Products and Markets	109
9.	Analyzing New Product Opportunities	125
10.	Planning the Proactive Product Development System: The Principles behind the Action	153

11.	Creating the Proactive Product Development System	167
12.	Experimentation and Rapid Prototyping	195
13.	From Pilot Production to Product Retirement: Managing the Post-Product Development Process	213
14.	Implementing Strategic Product Development	229

| *Appendix I.* | *New Product Decision Screen* | 237 |
| *Appendix II.* | *Strategic Plan Format* | 243 |

Bibliography — 261

Index — 265

Preface

This book is about the process of developing powerful products. Powerful products are new products that meet the strategic objectives set for them in terms of the following factors:

- Reaching the target market segment
- Meeting anticipated volume projections over the product life
- Providing the forecast contribution over the life of the product
- Contributing to the vitality and health of the company

Satisfying these objectives is challenging but by no means impossible. We can all identify companies from different countries that have a long string of powerful products. *Powerful Products* analyzes the new product development process and sets out a comprehensive system for improving a company's new product success rate.

The new product development process laid out in this book is based on a handful of simple propositions:

- The decision to produce a new product is a fundamental strategic decision and must be made at the highest levels of the company.
- The first decision to be made must be the selection of the target market segment.

- The product must satisfy user needs and expectations, but it must also satisfy some operational concerns.
- The new product development process must be executed quickly.
- The new product development process must actively involve the complete supply and distribution chain, not simply internal marketers, designers, and engineers.

Powerful Products springs from the authors' work with companies on three continents and from discussions with dissatisfied senior executives and managers from all functional areas in numerous manufacturing companies (and some service and high-tech companies). We found that new product development is a haphazard process in most companies because of lack of strategic input at the beginning of the process and because of strategic drift throughout the process. Compounding this haphazardness in companies is poor coordination among departments. We have seen companies with gifted designers, marketers who understand their markets, talented engineers, and knowledgeable manufacturers adept at producing quality products that nevertheless have a startlingly low rate of success with new products, partly because the various groups do not work effectively together.

This lack of integration is reflected in the books written on the topic. We have been impressed by the quality of the insights and the writing of the majority of the books on new product development that we have read, and from which we have learned. However, there is one disturbing but understandable characteristic of almost all the books—they are written for a specific cluster of operational managers, usually in one functional area. Hardly any are strategic, and almost none are both strategic and operational. Thus, they continue to reinforce the gulf between functional areas, even while exhorting, for example, multifunctional team approaches to product development.

We have also learned from observation and discussion that the process of developing product developers and managers of product development is sketchy and haphazard at best. Functional expertise, a good background in the industry, knowledge of critical customers, and an inquiring mind are important attributes of people involved in product development, but they are not enough. People involved as members of development teams would benefit greatly from instruction and coaching in teamwork, communication, strategy development and planning, project management, innovation, and the overall product development process. Managers of product development would benefit from a good understanding of leadership and the management of change.

To develop integrated product development approaches, organizations need tools that can be used by people in different functional areas, not by just one group alone. This book meets that need.

Powerful Products lays out a simple process to help strategic and operational managers handle the complexity of new product development. Because the problems in the product design process are managerial and organizational in nature, not technical, the book contains little technical detail or jargon. It is a tool for senior executives, team members, and managers, detailing a process that generates consistently successful products.

Organization of the Book

Powerful Products is organized along the general line of our new product development process, which has three major blocks of activities:

- Developing the corporate strategy, including getting the market segmentation right
- Developing product concepts that are appropriate for the target market segments
- Designing, manufacturing, and distributing the products

Most organizations start at the end of the list, assuming the first two items are agreed on or will be worked out later. Product design and development, therefore, becomes a lower-level activity in the organization and is only coincidentally successful. Too many companies end up spending too much time developing intriguing products for which there are no markets.

So this book starts at the top and works its way down. Chapter 1 provides an overview of the problems with existing new product development processes and outlines the activities an effective process has to be able to accomplish for new product development to be effective. Chapters 2 through 5 look at the many strategic issues, from segmenting target markets, to formulating product development strategies, to understanding the impact of senior management, customers, and corporate culture on the development of successful products.

Chapters 6 through 9 provide the operational underpinning for the new product development process. Identifying new product opportunities and mapping them into the current portfolio of competitive products and attractive markets is critical and carried out before even the first hint at design. And Chapters 10 through 13 develop the new product development system in detail, from obtaining specific customer data, to product design, manufacture, and launch, to product extension and retirement. Managing the process is also discussed, for that is a critical concern for the target audience.

Chapter 14 focuses on how to implement the overall process. A decision poorly implemented is virtually useless; you cannot manage what you cannot implement.

We hope this book proves an invaluable aid in your quest to develop powerful products.

Acknowledgments

We have profited tremendously from discussions with managers in many companies, and to single any out would be a disservice to the others. Our understanding of the issues and approaches to various aspects of new product development was deepened considerably by the wealth of excellent material available in the large number of books that deal with the subject, and we were privileged to discuss the issues with some of the authors. All were unfailingly courteous and encouraging of our efforts, and many gave us new ideas to consider.

Powerful Products would probably never have come to pass without the influence of Frank Bacon, Jerry McCarthy, and the folks at Planned Innovation. We owe more to these two remarkable gentlemen than we could possibly detail here. Working with them proved to be a very rewarding, enlightening, and profitable experience. We are similarly indebted to Charles Owen for his influence, particularly in Chapter 11. Steve Eldersveld is responsible for the witty and poignant cartoons scattered throughout the book. Having spent more than a decade in pursuit of new products, he knows of what he draws.

Powerful Products is full of examples gleaned from successful companies, some named and others not. Most of these companies we have worked with in some form; in other instances we are reporting what has already been published. It would not be possible to write a book such as this without good examples and the inspiration they provide, and we cannot overstate the debt we owe to the managers with whom we have worked. We have learned much from discussing and analyzing their successes.

We realize that this book is a new product and is the first test of our new product development process. So it gives us great pleasure to thank first of all the selected representatives of the target market segment who cheerfully discussed the concept and then read various drafts of the text. We also acknowledge the work of Robert Linsenman, our literary agent, who provided us with insights into the needs and expectations of publishers and then convinced AMACOM that we were worth the risk. We also are delighted to acknowledge the support and detailed guidance provided to us by Ray O'Connell and the team at AMACOM, who made integrating the creative and technical so much a delight, rather than a drudgery.

We also have two special boosters and supporters to thank, two people busier than we are who provided support at the appropriate time, who understood the hold the project had on us, and who graciously kept our collective nose to the grindstone. Lynnette and Debra, thanks for being part of our lives and for being the special friends you are. The writing partnership is not two people, but four.

We would appreciate having any errors of fact or interpretation pointed out to us, so that appropriate corrections can be made.

Powerful Products

1

Strategic Product Development

As we enter the new millennium, companies face an increasingly competitive environment and increasing pressure to perform. This new era will be one in which each will be challenged to provide more new, exciting, innovative, and cost-effective products than ever before.

The last few decades of the twentieth century brought to the Western world a new awakening, sparked by the 1973 oil crisis. The Japanese proved emphatically that there was more than one way to conduct business. Vulnerabilities in the "common wisdom" of the West (such as "quality costs the customer more," or "the customer should not expect much real choice," and slow service as normal) were paraded for everyone to see. Fortunately, the crisis turned out to be something of a blessing in disguise. The Chinese symbol for "crisis" is also the symbol for "opportunity," and the oil crisis gave Western companies the opportunity to create change. Most responded to the opportunity.

The fear of—and respect for—the Japanese economic machine was almost palpable. We began taking our own advice and administering corrective medicine. And it worked. Aided in no small part by flaws in the economies of the Pacific Rim countries, the West rebounded with great vigor.

After the Japanese experience, Western business rallied to the call with the motto "Faster, better, cheaper." At the close of the twentieth century we are again riding high. However, we have done it mostly with "faster and cheaper" products. The near future will inevitably bring with it a renewed emphasis on "better" performance. Price reductions without simultaneous improvement in performance, design, feature selection, availability, or service will no longer suffice.

New and exciting products will be demanded in all sectors as individual consumers and business customers alike tire of "yesterday's products cheaper." Cost reduction will continue, of course, but a focus on reducing costs will be displaced by product differentiation and superiority as the preferred path to growth and premium return.

Certainly, this is already happening in industries like personal computers, biotechnology, telecommunications, and many Internet services. It is, however, somewhat natural in these fast-paced industries to keep a flow of better products coming through the pipeline. It has been a somewhat less natural response in those industries that provide the more mundane products, which make up the vast majority of the sales in our economy.

Many companies have zeroed in on cost reduction and speed because they appeared to be safer and less costly than adopting a value-focused policy. Many of those companies have found considerable success doing so. But it is definitely possible to create and introduce products that do all three simultaneously. It is not necessary to settle for half a loaf. Innovative, commercially successful products are not just a game of trial and error consuming huge amounts of wasted investment.

> *Better, not just cheaper, products will be the key to success in the coming decades.*

> *New products do not have to be "higher risk" than cost-reducing existing products.*

New product development should be viewed strategically; that is, conceived and funded to achieve specific objectives in both the marketplace and the corporate competitive portfolio. To do so successfully requires a balance of three factors. If these become unbalanced or if one is missing entirely, the probability of success declines rapidly.

Three Critical Elements

Successful new product development requires the effective performance and balance of three activities critical to new product success. The key to success lies in performing each element properly.

1. Strategic processes must specifically address the effective management of product development assets.
2. The most important decision any company must make is the selection of its target markets, the specific customers it wishes to serve. This requires a workable, accurate market segmentation model.
3. If successes are to be repeatable, there must be a disciplined, structured product development process that ensures that the development investment is always performing in direct support of corporate goals and strategies.

Powerful Products shows how these three key elements can be successfully implemented in your company and how they can be effectively integrated through the proper application of strategic information and principles.

Defining Success

Before we can begin developing successful products, we must understand what we mean by "successful." When someone refers to a "successful" product, that judgment results from the assumptions or perspective of the speaker. If the speaker were a production line foreman, a successful product might be one that lends itself to efficient manufacture. To a sales manager it might be a product that sells easily and in large quantities, permitting the sales department to exceed its goals.

A design engineer might find a product that incorporated considerable innovation and ingenuity to increase performance to new levels to be a highly successful design effort. An industrial designer might view a product with superb ergonomics that represented aesthetic harmony to be a considerable achievement. A research engineer might consider the harnessing of a completely new technology in an innovative and productive way to be a genuine success.

A young couple walking into a mass merchandiser might find a "ready to assemble" entertainment center for $229.00 to be a genuine bargain, representing attractive design and high value. A middle-aged professional couple might be equally enthusiastic about a small reproduction Chippendale piecrust table at $4,200. A graphic designer might see a new graphics software package offering greatly improved control with new features as a stunning success.

Given the criteria that each observer is applying to his or her definition of the "successful" product, these are all successful products. Such diversity of criteria among various interest groups makes it essential to create a common working definition of precisely what constitutes a successful product. Such a definition should be available for every development effort.

For clarity of discussion, this book focuses on one particular type of business, making four assumptions:

> *"I don't know the key to success, but the key to failure is trying to please everybody."*
> *—Bill Cosby*

> *Establishing the criteria for commercial success is a key responsibility of executive management.*

1. *It is a commercial enterprise (as opposed to a nonprofit organization)*. For any commercial enterprise, profit is essential to survival. Obvious as it may seem, product profit is not negotiable. Or at least it shouldn't be. It is amazing, however, how every company encounters some very creative and sometimes persuasive arguments for unprofitable products:

- "We can get the margins up later."
- "We need it to broaden the line."
- "Our costs will come down in time."
- "We risk losing all our other business with this client unless we make this item at a loss."
- "We'll make it up on the other items in the system."
- "If we don't make it, our competitors will."
- "It will attract new customers, so we'll get other, more profitable business."
- "This product is low-margin, but it will utilize excess production capacity."
- "Our methods of costing understate the real profitability."

It is neither necessary nor desirable to produce unprofitable products. Period. It should always be possible to create a profitable portfolio of products when clear targets are addressed by means of a disciplined and structured process. If the development process is not directly supportive of a strategic focus, in the context of an effective means of isolating profitable customers, then success—repeatable success—is extremely unlikely.

> *In a commercial enterprise, it is commercial success that ensures survival.*

> *Poor product profitability is a self-inflicted wound.*

2. *The reader's primary business is manufacturing.* This assumption is a simple device to enable greater clarity. Attempting to write a book for every conceivable product type, from insurance to heavy construction equipment, in an effort to increase readership (and sales) usually results in a more muddled message. We seek to be clear; hence, we address manufacturing situations here, even though the principles are generally applicable to a wide variety of situations.

3. *The industry is competitive (nonmonopolistic).* The more competitive the industry, the more demanding is the need for effective strategies, products, and innovation. A monopoly will conceal a lot of poor decisions. The consequences of a highly competitive marketplace are quickly and severely felt at the individual competitor level.

4. *Some business and product development needs are more important than others.* Because there are obviously many different needs a product can satisfy, it is prudent and useful to establish a hierarchy of needs to guide the efforts of product development. Some needs are more important than others if a company is to be successful and profitable. To this end, it is essential that management be clear about why a new product is being developed (its strategic role) and who the target customer is.

Product Success Versus Commercial Success

"Product success" can be achieved on many levels. New technologies, new features, improved performance, lower cost, better design, and improved durability are all examples of product success. These are achievements that are usually hard earned at the product development team level and are deserving of credit.

"Commercial success" may be a very different sort of thing. Commercial success has two components—acceptable margin and acceptable sales volume (see Figure 1-1). High-margin products that generate few sales contribute little to the business and will consume time and resources better devoted to more productive endeavors. Products with high sales volume but with little or no margin are not as benign. The impact of these profit killers

Figure 1-1. Formula for commercial success.

> Commercial Success = acceptable margin
> × acceptable sales volume

can be devastating. They must be replaced with products capable of "paying their own way."

For commercial success to occur, then, the products must be profitable. Each product should meet "target profitability" goals. Unprofitable products cannot produce commercial success, no matter how "cool" or innovative they may be. So, why do almost all manufacturers have such a bevy of underperforming products in their portfolio? Clearly, there is a need for new solutions to the underperforming portfolio. The potential for improved earnings is enormous.

Creating Competitive Strategy

Companies compete for the sales dollars that ultimately pay the salaries and provide for the future of their employees. To see the marketplace as a benign place where "there's enough business for everyone" may sound very generous and high-minded, but, at the very best, it results in a static view of a changing situation. At worst, it makes a company ill prepared to compete when the business environment does become difficult and demanding. Prudent businesspeople always assume that they will have to earn (win) all the business they get.

The following model for creating competitive strategy entails three "levels" of activity: the strategic, the tactical, and the

> *Developing the right perspective on competition has a great deal to do with the ability to succeed.*

operational. It gives a rather narrowly focused view to help you "envision" a more effective approach to developing more successful products. Here, it is only intended to show how the three levels are inseparable in the creation of high-performance products. This framework is expanded on in later chapters. Developing the necessary internal skills to implement such an approach is also discussed in subsequent chapters.

The Strategic Level

Selection of the target markets in which your company will compete is a strategic decision of the utmost importance. Nearly all companies receive some business from outside their target segments. The key is not to confuse this "overflow" business with new opportunity. To do so will inevitably diffuse the hard-earned focus that is so difficult to achieve. If you don't select the best customer targets around which to structure your business, then pricing will be a problem as marketing and sales try to compensate for low-profit customers. Strategy and golf are in some ways similar, as can be seen in Figure 1-2.

Pricing is another important strategic concern. If a product does not support a satisfactory margin by means of superior and innovative design, engineering, manufacture, and value, then the sales department will always be trying to sell it for less in an effort to achieve acceptable volume. Also, if the sales department has no input or influence over pricing, you stand to lose considerable competitive flexibility, and inevitably profit opportunities are lost. Many pricing problems can be traced back to flawed selection of target markets, which results in trying to sell the wrong products to the wrong customers. It becomes an insidious cycle.

> *When a company is serving the wrong customers (i.e., those it is ill suited to serve), these customers are almost always low-profit customers, and the products aimed at them are poor-performing products.*

Figure 1-2. Similarities between scratch golf and strategic prowess.

> **Scratch golf and strategic prowess have much in common:**
> - The basic idea behind each is pretty simple.
> - Nobody has ever been born with either skill.
> - Real skill comes only with a lot of hard work.
> - Not many people ever become really good at either.
> - Finally, it's immeasurably easier to be a great player if nobody actually gets to watch you play.

Strategy is a learned skill, and there are time-honored and proven principles that govern its development and application. These principles are based on the premise of an adversary. Strategy is about competing—to win. In the context of this book, the principles of strategy are engaged in the confrontation that occurs in the marketplace between competitive adversaries. The strategic activities discussed here are thus directed toward overcoming market adversaries to secure profitable sales with profitable products to clearly targeted customers. This understanding is central to creating successful products.

The relationship of the strategic to the operational and tactical, shown in Figure 1-3, is key to organizing for successful product development. It is common to view goal setting and strategy development as proper activities for management, but it is less common to assign customer targeting to the executive group. Customer targeting is usually viewed as the legitimate role of the marketing department. However, because profitable sales are the engine driving the entire organization, selection of the target markets is one of the most important and strategic challenges. Precisely whom is the firm attempting to serve? When this central question is relegated exclusively to the mar-

> *Planning and strategy are not the same thing . . . despite what the dictionary says!*

Figure 1-3. Levels of strategic activity.

LEVEL	STRATEGIC	OPERATIONAL	TACTICAL
WHO	Executive	Engineering Marketing Industrial Design Manufacturing	Sales Customer Service
ACTIVITY	○ Selection of target segments ○ Goal setting ○ Strategy development ○ Pricing	○ Developing new products ○ Producing the product or service ○ Supporting sales efforts ○ Pricing	○ Getting the order ○ Developing accounts ○ Servicing customers ○ Pricing

keting department and is not the province of combined executive decision making, the company is likely to suffer from a blurred focus.

For an organization to be unclear on such a central issue is to encourage confusion and costly inefficiency throughout the organization. Our experience suggests that virtually all firms can benefit from a clearer definition of their target markets. Do any of these sound familiar?

- SALES: "We're working as hard as we can, but until we get some new products we may not be able to meet our goals."
- MANUFACTURING: "Sales seems to sell all the products that don't make any money. Why don't they sell the high-margin products?"
- ENGINEERING: "We spend all this effort developing really great ideas that we can't get marketing or sales to pursue."
- MARKETING: Manufacturing can't get its costs down, so we're expected to work miracles with overpriced products!"

Strategic Product Development

- HEADQUARTERS: "Why can't the sales department just sell what we make rather than always want something else?" "What we need are some *salesmen* instead of order takers!"
- ENGINEERING: "First, sales wants a low-priced product. We give it to them, and now they say that's not what they meant. Why can't they make up their mind!"
- SALES: "We still need lower-priced product."

Wherever such complaints are heard, one can bet the customer targets are unclear. Just as definitions of success depend on the perspective of the viewer, the same is true with complaints. Most are somewhat right—and somewhat wrong—and progress grinds to a halt while each group recites its favorite mantra. Each group is making different assumptions. Getting clarity begins with the strategic selection of precisely whom the company exists to serve. If it's not spelled out, everyone has to guess—and they often guess differently.

The Tactical Level

Let's jump forward to the other end of the business, the tactical level. The tactical requirements of competing pivot around the selling and servicing activity, whether these functions are conducted by an internal sales force, by retailers or distributors, or by some other combination. Tactical activities are "front line" activities, involving contact with the customer. But making a sale is almost never the exclusive realm of the sales department. The sales department cannot sell products without help and support. Its success depends on the strategic and operational activities that precede the actual sales. The sales function is hobbled if strategic and operational activities are not effectively implemented.

The sales department is responsible, however, for develop-

> *Tactics and strategy are two sides of the same coin. Both are necessary.*

ing the sales tactics necessary for sales success. The promotion department, working closely with the sales department, is responsible for advertising and promotion tactics. Managing, supporting, and motivating distributors or retailers may be a sales responsibility, or possibly the responsibility of a separate but closely allied department, but however organized, these three functions (sales, promotion, and customer service) comprise the essence of the tactical competitive activity of the company.

Although the sales department is generally where problems manifest themselves most clearly, because it operates on the front line with customers, failure of products to sell as forecast is rarely the fault of the sales department alone. If the target markets are not clear, and the products not targeted, there is relatively little the salespeople can do to improve the situation, even if they *are* selling in the target market. The most common cry is for a lower price in the desperate effort to entice customers to buy. But the problem usually goes deeper than price, which, although a symptom, is not usually the cause of the sales problem. Lowering the price is often just a means of trying to entice customers to buy products that do not suit their needs, tastes, desires, or means. It is a simple attempt to fit a square peg into a round hole.

There is a common misconception that formulating and implementing strategy is somehow an "intellectually superior" calling to formulating tactics. Tactical elements are every bit as essential to success, and as demanding to master, however, as the strategic. Tactical activities merely take place on the front lines, usually in direct contact with the customer.

The Operational Level

Most business literature seems to ignore the operational level, typically discussing only the strategic and the tactical. It is a serious omission, causing considerable confusion in the day-to-day world of business. The operational level bridges the strategic and the tactical. Operational activities are those that enable and support the tactical. It is a common axiom in the army that it takes nine noncombatant soldiers to support one combat soldier. In business it is almost assuredly an even higher ratio.

Because the emphasis here is on successful new products, in the operational level we include manufacturing, marketing, engineering, and design. (If management is responsible for the strategic direction of the company, and the sales and service functions are responsible for the tactical, then clearly engineering, manufacturing, marketing, and design fall into the operational level.)

For most manufacturers the product (including both the tangible and intangible elements) is *the* source of revenue. This is where the entirety of perceived value to the customer resides. From a new product development focus, then, the operational level is where most of the activity will take place. These are the functional departments from which the multidisciplinary product team members are generally drawn.

Integrating the Three Levels

There are critical decisions to be made at each of the three levels. Those made by executive management fall under "strategic planning" or "strategic management." When similar decisions are made by the sales and promotion departments, they are called "tactics" to differentiate between the nature and urgency of the content. The operational level includes the bulk of the day-to-day decisions required to keep the business machine running. Operational decisions often involve product development.

If no distinction is made among the various levels, then it becomes difficult to coordinate a stream of successful new products. If the process becomes internally competitive, rather than mutually supportive, little will be accomplished without gargantuan effort.

In addition, the effects of nonperformance are cumulative. Because the executive group gets to define the rules of the game, it has to do its part first. Should it fail to define the rules or

> *The strategic, tactical, and operational levels all have important decisions to make.*

articulate goals and strategies, the next group will be compelled to develop its own to fill the gaps. Similarly, if the operational group fails, the sales group will find itself confronted with unachievable goals because the products and support levels are inadequate to entice customers. The sales group then suggests lowering the price, and the finger pointing begins. If the operational group succeeds, precisely the reverse happens, and that's exactly what you want to achieve.

Effective Product Development

If you accept that the overall goal of the company is commercial success, and that each of the levels of the strategy-making process have different but essential roles in ensuring successful products, then you can develop a process capable of achieving that goal.

Figure 1-4 lists the key elements in the process in a roughly linear sequence. The sequence lists key functions or tasks that need to be performed without regard to the internal organization or department responsible. At this juncture, only the major functions are listed. More functions are provided in the following chapters.

The purpose of a structured process is simple. It is to ensure that the necessary steps are taken, all the necessary questions are asked, and all the product success criteria are met. A good process ensures that we can repeat our successes again and again. If the successes are intermixed with more than a few disappointments, the process is almost always part of the problem.

First Things First

The first requirement is to develop an effective market segmentation model. If you have a model that satisfies the need for accuracy and clarity, then one large hurdle is already overcome. If you are even a little uncertain as to what your target market is, then stop now and develop one that will satisfy the requirements of strategy development and product development. To

Figure 1-4. Product development process overview.

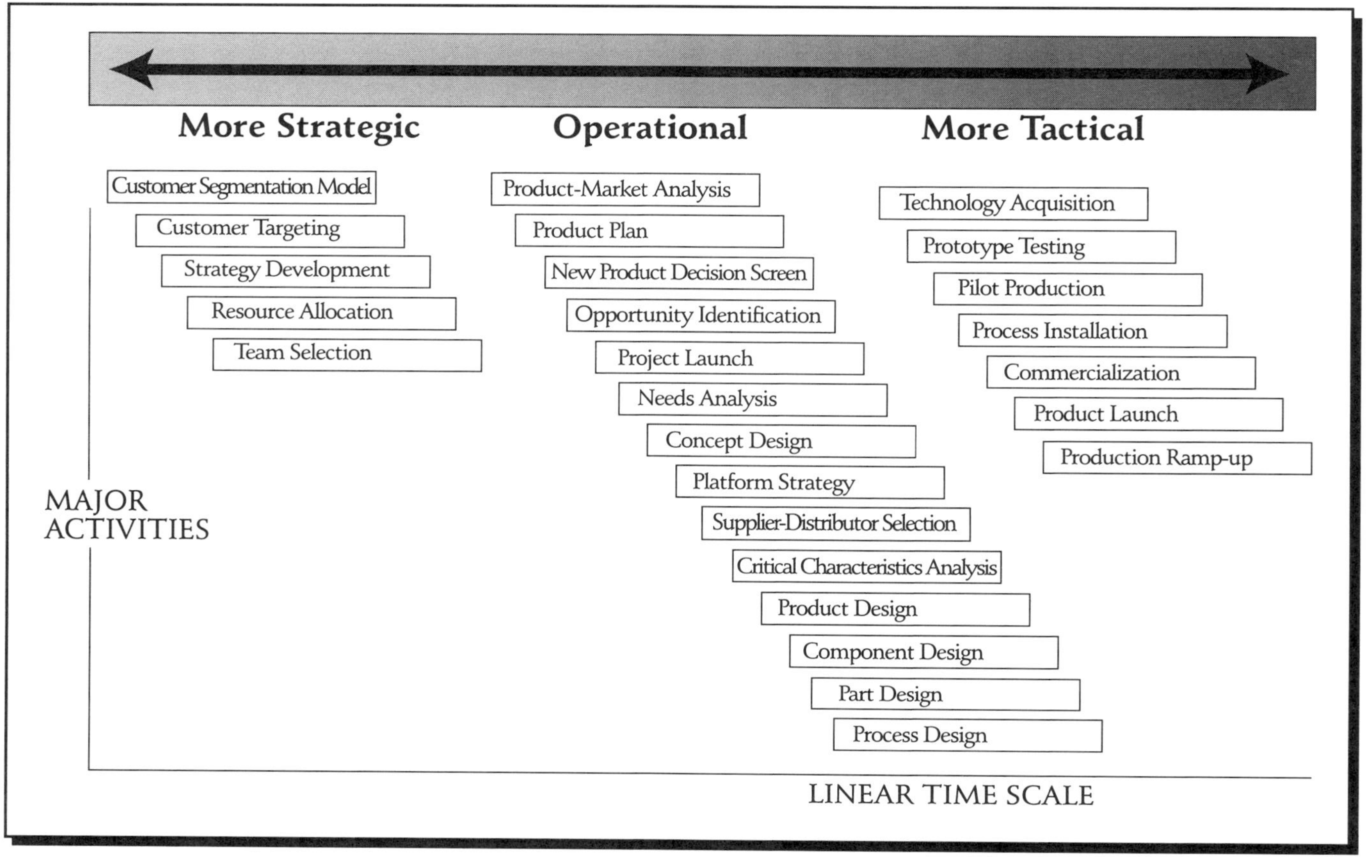

More Strategic	Operational	More Tactical
Customer Segmentation Model	Product-Market Analysis	Technology Acquisition
Customer Targeting	Product Plan	Prototype Testing
Strategy Development	New Product Decision Screen	Pilot Production
Resource Allocation	Opportunity Identification	Process Installation
Team Selection	Project Launch	Commercialization
	Needs Analysis	Product Launch
	Concept Design	Production Ramp-up
	Platform Strategy	
	Supplier-Distributor Selection	
	Critical Characteristics Analysis	
	Product Design	
	Component Design	
	Part Design	
	Process Design	

MAJOR ACTIVITIES

LINEAR TIME SCALE

begin without the clarity of focus offered by such information is to virtually guarantee and institutionalize fuzzy thinking even before the first dollar is invested in product development. To presume that you can bypass the effort required to develop such an understanding is to risk wasting much or all of your development investment.

Once a strategic segmentation model is developed, there needs to be a conscious decision as to precisely which segments the firm is going to target. This process needs to be undertaken at the highest levels and can be considerably more time-consuming than you might imagine. But it's essential. Clarity begins at the top.

Before any development is even contemplated, the executive group needs to examine and analyze the competitive situation relative to the target segments. Management needs to know why the company is successful in certain segments and why they are less successful in other areas. A conscious and rigorous effort is required to set the strategic direction focusing on specific targeted segments. The strategy development effort should specifically address how the product (development) resource will be utilized to compete in the marketplace.

The development process should include sufficient structure to ensure that the team covers all the necessary bases and does not unintentionally deviate from the strategic purpose intended by executive management.

The central premise of this book is that it is necessary to integrate these three key elements as seamlessly as possible. When a company brings the three elements together, problems seem to evaporate, cooperation is commonplace, and satisfied customers become the norm. Product failures are rare. Sales and profits increase in ways not before possible. Development costs decline substantially because false starts are all but eliminated. Products come to market much faster, further improving market performance. Everyone enjoys the satisfaction of a job well done and the pride of being on a winning team, so interdepartmental rivalry declines dramatically, and cooperation thrives.

The average manufacturer can probably gain more from improving performance in the product development area than in any other.

Summary

For all its challenges, successful new product development is both achievable and repeatable. Most new product disasters are the direct result of a failure to properly integrate accurate information about customer needs and wants with strategic market selection. Repeatability ensues from a structured process that permits teams to succeed again and again. Accordingly, a structured process requires some level of corporate discipline.

We have seen that commercial success requires both acceptable profit margin and acceptable volume levels. Commercial success is made much more difficult when executive management fails to carefully and clearly select and define those target markets the company will seek to serve. Furthermore, selecting target markets finds a tremendous aid in the availability of a strategic market segmentation model. A good model is both specific and accurate.

Competitive actions that are guided by an understanding of strategic principles are inevitably the most consistently successful. Competition is inherently adversarial, and the principles of strategy are likewise adversarial in nature.

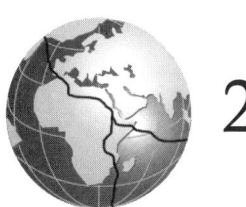# 2

The Genesis of New Products

Where do new products come from? How are they originated? What is the initiating step or activity? Depending on whom you ask, you will get different answers. Some common answers are these:

- "We solicit new product ideas from our employees."
- "Customer requests for new or special products spark most of our new products."
- "Our research and development department is responsible for coming up with new product concepts."
- "We're really lucky to have Harry Belknap. He (the resident mad inventor) comes up with nearly all our new products."
- "We follow the new developments in technology to get ideas for new products."
- "Our engineers are really good. We actually have more new product concepts than we can develop."
- "We study competitors and match their offerings, aiming for a lower price."

Taken together, these answers seem to suggest that good ideas for new products can come from anywhere. Actually, each of the methods produces "solutions looking for a problem," or stated a bit differently, "products looking for a market." Even to

> *"Good ideas can come from anywhere."* Maybe, but don't bet on it. Sometimes good enough *ideas don't come at all.*

the untrained eye this approach looks to have it a bit backward. Shouldn't one identify opportunities, *then* develop innovative and elegant solutions?

Although some very successful products have resulted from the aforementioned sources, such methods are inherently unreliable at producing commercial success. What is to ensure that any of the ideas available at any given time are really appropriate to enhancing competitiveness in the sectors most favorable to a company's success?

The key difference between a skilled fisherman and someone who just fishes can be clearly identified. The skilled fisherman understands a great deal about his prey. When seeing a lake for the first time, the skilled fisherman knows that less than 10 percent of the area of the lake contains any fish at all. For reasons of cover and proximity to food, about 90 percent of every lake is barren of fish. The serious fisherman will take the first opportunity to purchase a topographical map of the lake to see what it looks like under the surface.

Second, the skilled fisherman knows that different species of fish have different preferences for food, cover, and company. Our fisherman also knows the most likely places to find the specific species he's fishing for.

Third, our hypothetical fisherman knows that different species feed on different prey at different times of the year, mostly due to availability. He will then consider what is available for his preferred species, and select his bait accordingly.

Also, our fisherman knows that certain species are more likely to be actively feeding at different times of the day: Some prefer to feed at night, others feed more randomly.

It's easy to see why those who "just go fishing" and do not consider the factors that will, in fact, determine their success usually fail to catch much. Yes, once in a while they will stumble onto a feeding school of fish when they happen to have the right bait, but this casual success just provides a false signal. When they go back and try the same thing again, they catch nothing, and consider it just another of the mysteries of fishing.

Here might be a good place to insert the hoary old story of the two novice fishermen who rented a boat to go fishing. They stumbled onto a school of fish, and had the best mornings fishing ever. While motoring back to the harbor, one of the fishermen wondered aloud how they might find precisely the same spot on the following day. "That's easy," his companion replied, "I put a cross on the side of the boat at the exact spot where I let down my line." "That's stupid," said the first, "how do you know we'll get the same boat tomorrow?"

Too many attempts to repeat product development success depends on capturing the same superficial characteristics that were apparent when our one major success occurred. And most of us will miss the boat.

Most markets look much like the surface of the lake. You can't see what's underneath. The first need is to get a map of the lake (a strategic market segmentation model). Then we can begin learning more about the characteristics of our target customers. Strategic product development must begin at the top of the organization, and take substance in the form of clear customer targets and skillfully developed corporate competitive product strategies.

Information Requirements

Initiating the development of a new product unleashes a flood of questions requiring answers. The ultimate success of the forthcoming product depends almost entirely on how apt these questions are and how well they are answered.

Regardless of the genesis of the proposed new product, the questions and answers required are essentially the same. Whether the project originates with an idea from the engineering department, a possible opportunity proposed by sales, or a new concept developed by marketing, the information required to methodically proceed is essentially identical.

As noted in Chapter 1, each level of the organization (strategic, tactical, and operational) has a different role and thus has a different view of its information needs.

Asking the Right Questions

Information technology has vastly increased the amount of data we can manipulate in very short time intervals. This new capability has prompted breakthroughs of immense importance. In many instances, unfortunately, the information overload has actually made progress more difficult through a glut of extraneous data. A huge quantity of irrelevant data is not an improvement. It is not a substitute for the ability (i.e., the developed skill) to ask the right questions.

And the "right" questions are not always obvious. If they were, there wouldn't be so many product failures. As noted in Chapter 1, the purpose of the commercial enterprise is to compete in its chosen marketplace for the purpose of generating profit. Therefore, a fundamental information structure geared specifically to support that purpose is required.

Because product development is such a key element in the success or failure of the manufacturer, the information required for competitive success is part and parcel of the product development effort. When the purpose is to compete, market information is an essential element. There are several key information requirements:

- The information necessary to ensure successful new products must encompass several "levels" (i.e., strategic, tactical, operational).
- The information must suit the different purposes to which it will be applied at each level.
- The information needs must flow from the strategic to the operational to the tactical—not the reverse. Trying to ad-

> *The capacity to process a large amount of data is no substitute for asking the right question.*

dress the information needed in the reverse order results in confusion and frustration.
- For the system to function smoothly, the strategic market information must be preeminent. It must come first because it serves to focus the remainder of the information required.

Strategic Support of Product Development

A critical executive function is the development of corporate strategy. If this responsibility is not executed with skill, those responsible for creating the right products at the right price and at the right time will find the difficulty of their job increased immeasurably.

In the context of product development, there are several key requirements that must be satisfied by the executive management group. No one else can satisfy these fundamental needs.

- A clear vision of what business the company is in
- Selection of the "target markets" the company seeks to serve
- Delineation of the strategic role of product development (i.e., strategies)
- Allocation of sufficient resources to achieve product-intensive strategies
- Creation of a new product "decision screen" to guide new product efforts

The critical information required to fulfill these responsibilities is market knowledge. To make the best decisions, executives need an accurate picture of the entire market (or markets) in question, not just those sectors in which the company currently participates. At the strategic level the challenge is to select the

> *Strategic direction is the most important role of the executive.*

> *Every business needs a vehicle for targeting those customers it wants to serve.*

best business opportunities to pursue, not just to restate the business traditionally pursued. It is necessary to cast a wide net, then make the most attractive selections from a large enough universe.

The strategic market segmentation model is an invaluable corporate asset because it defines the universe from which so many critical corporate decisions are taken. Companies that have failed to formalize their "view" of their marketplace usually have a history of sporadic and inconsistent performance. How a company sees its marketplace is the most fundamental and elemental knowledge in the company.

When this fundamental knowledge is not formalized, all employees are compelled to make their own "working assumptions" and create their own market model (some would call it a "mind map") so they can make the decisions they need to make. These individual understandings of the market are drawn from internal discussion, training, opinions of those who have "been around," and so on. Bits and pieces of market information are combined with the person's individual experience and—violà!—each employee forms a view of the market. The problem, of course, is that each is a little different from the others.

Executives, usually because they are among the more experienced employees, may feel quite comfortable with their own personal "mind map" of their marketplace. But each executive's view is also a little different.

A good strategic market segmentation model should:

- Describe the entire market, not just the segments in which the company currently participates.
- Encompass all of the four primary means of segmenting: product type, customer type (demographics), functional needs, geography.

- Provide clean segments (i.e., homogeneous within and heterogeneous between segments).
- Facilitate "targeted" strategies.

Figure 2-1 shows how market information forms the basis of several critical executive activities (i.e., those that fall within the purview of the strategic). With the strategic market segmentation model in place, executives can fulfill their strategic responsibilities more effectively because the question of how much business comes from where is always apparent. Focus becomes possible. With the strategic map of the battleground in place, people at the next level can proceed in a much more focused manner as they execute the strategies outlined by the executive group. The strategic market segmentation model is discussed in more detail in Chapter 4.

Market Knowledge Required at the Operations Level

Once the "corporate level" strategic decisions are made to provide direction and focus to the organization, the operations team can grab the ball and run. Usually, they don't run very far before finding they need information as well—and it's not the same information created for the strategic decisions. But the operations folks are not starting from scratch in their information search. Far from it. In fact, their information search can be narrowed immensely because the targeting done at the strategic level should have eliminated most of the universe of data with respect to any particular project. Their search is narrowed.

Figure 2-2 shows how market information applied at the strategic decision level guides the new product development project at the operational level.

The information needs of the project team formed to pursue a specific new product are quite specific. Unlike the executive team members, who needed a snapshot of the entire market or industry, the project team must be much more focused. The scope and target of the project is already defined. But project team members require precise information about the needs of the target customer segment if they are to design a successful product. For our purposes we call the needed specific project

(text continues on page 28)

Figure 2-1. Applying market knowledge at the strategic level.

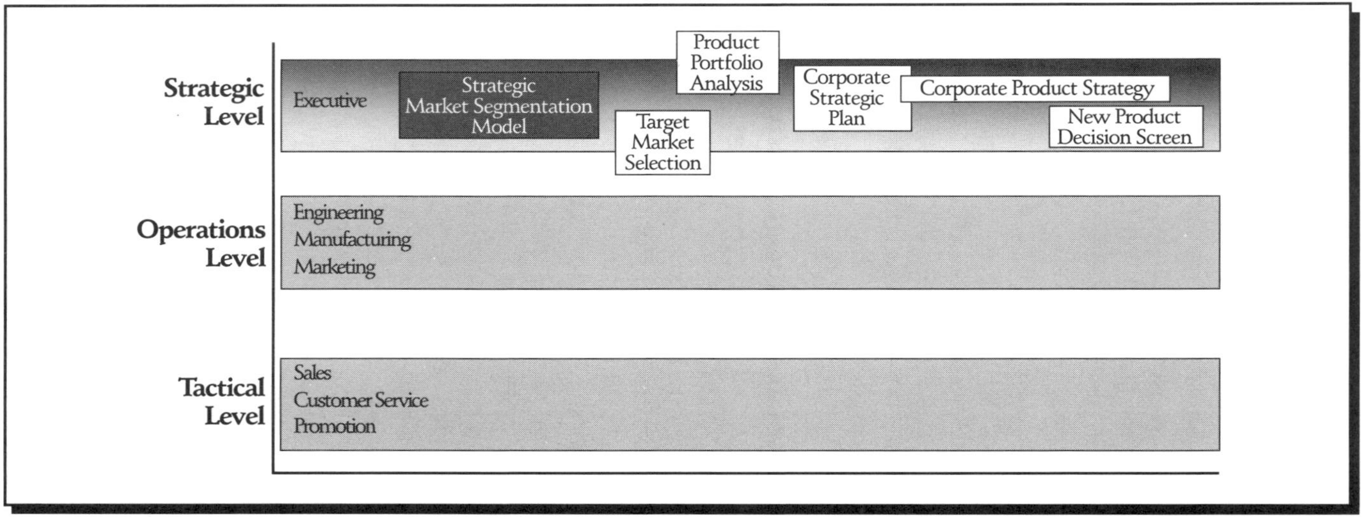

Strategic Level	Strategic Market Segmentation Model — Target Market Selection — Product Portfolio Analysis — Corporate Strategic Plan — Corporate Product Strategy — New Product Decision Screen Executive
Operations Level	Engineering Manufacturing Marketing
Tactical Level	Sales Customer Service Promotion

Figure 2-2. Applying market knowledge at the operations level.

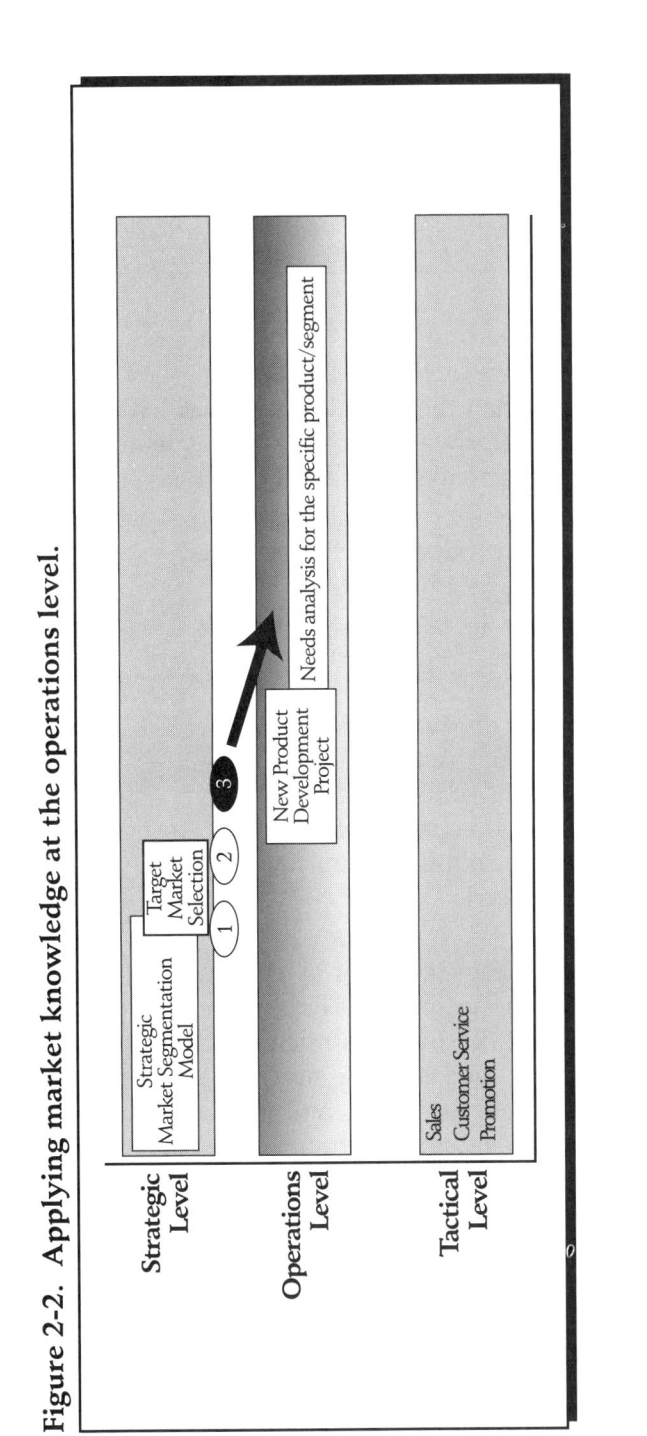

> *Rather than beginning with specific functional product needs, the strategic issues must come first.*

information "needs analysis." The requirements may not be limited to purely "functional" needs, but they should be much more focused than they would have been without the benefit of the clear targets provided by the strategy team.

The "needs analysis" typically includes information about:

- How the product is or will be used
- Technical requirements
- Who specifically uses the product
- Availability requirements
- Key features
- Durability requirements
- Service requirements
- Economics of use
- Information content of product
- Warranty requirements
- Unmet needs

This may seem like a lot of additional information, but remember that the universe of data to be examined has been reduced dramatically by the strategic targeting process. Without the benefit of such focus, the needs analysis process inevitably becomes diffused, imprecise, and overgeneralized.

Products developed without benefit of rigorous needs analysis frequently include features that design team members *think* are valuable, but in reality the ultimate customer is unwilling to pay for. There's an old saying that it's easy to sell Cadillacs to Chevy buyers—one merely has to sell them at the Chevy price! Such is the case with the product with unvalued features. The product usually finds a price at which someone will buy it, but because of the unnecessary features the margin has just gone down. This is how a lot of products become the low-margin performers. Furthermore, without sufficiently clear targets it's easy for the design group to omit key features, causing the same outcome. With a specific, targeted project, however, the team can include only those features that are indeed valued by the target segment and ensure that important features are not omitted.

Without stringent needs analysis, the producer ends up "fixing" the product by redesigning and reengineering the faulty item to either add or delete features or functions missed in the initial development. This trial-and-error approach to satisfying market needs amounts to developing every product twice—or three times, or even more. This is an expensive strategy. This is an insane strategy.

Tactical Market Information Needs

At the tactical level, information requirements are somewhat outside the scope of our enquiry; but because the product development team benefits from a tactical understanding, we'll fill in this level just a bit. The tactical level by its very nature is marked by a sense of urgency and detail more typical of day-to-day sales, service, and promotion activities. These needs we will call "market research," because this is the bread-and-butter business of the market researcher.

Market researchers are concerned with such matters as corporate identity, name recognition, product satisfaction, customer confidence, sales lead generation, competitive information, market penetration, and so on. Standard market research

> *The needs analysis is the focus of the development team.*

> *Market research is the primary vehicle for obtaining tactical market information.*

Figure 2-3. Applying market knowledge at the tactical level.

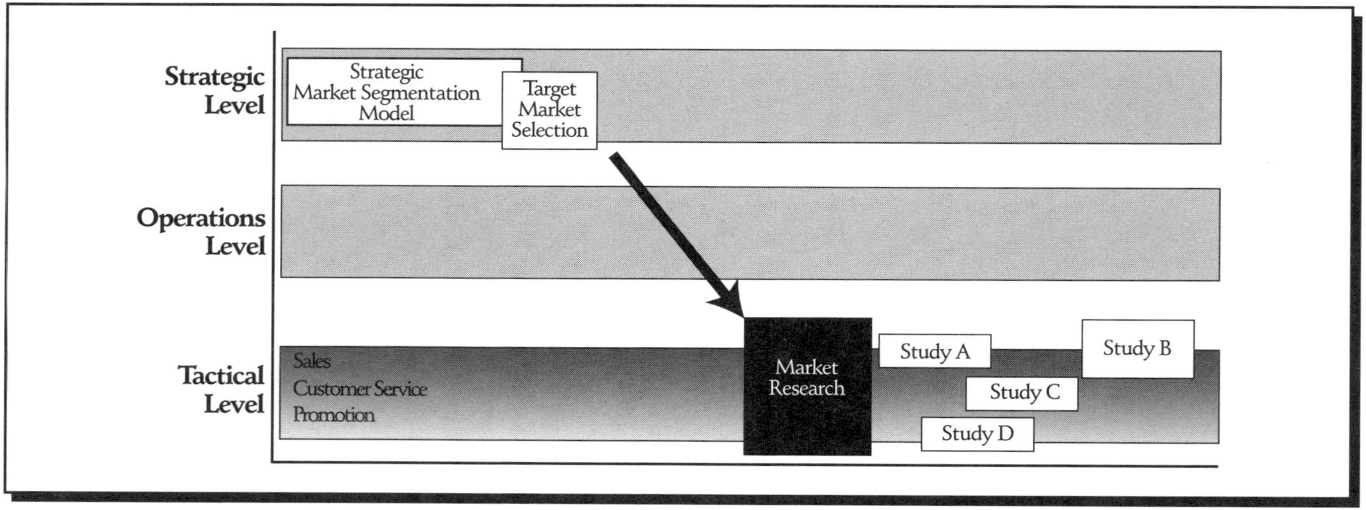

techniques work best here, because that's primarily what these methods are designed to do.

Currently available market research methods do not work very well for segmenting markets, however, particularly industrial markets. The needs analysis requirements of the product development team are best done by the team itself if at all possible.

As shown in Figure 2-3, specific market research projects in the selected segments are needed to guide ongoing advertising, promotional, and service activities at the tactical level. Even at the tactical level, market research benefits from the focus provided by the strategic market segmentation model. Advertising and promotion activities have clear targets, and additional information about those targets can be obtained much more effectively and at less cost with the strategic market segmentation model in place. Sales lead generation and follow-up research are similarly more easily focused with targeted segments.

Summary

As we've seen, new product ideas may come from many places, but as we've shown, it is usually a mistake to put much faith in "random innovation" as a consistent source for new products. We clearly advocate that new products should be primarily the result of "applied strategy." Development dollars directed specifically to supporting specific corporate strategies will outperform random innovation in almost every case.

There are three distinct strategic levels in the development process. These are the strategic, the tactical, and the operational levels. Each requires different information to function effectively. To flow smoothly, the product development process should proceed first from the strategic level and with the benefit of a well-crafted strategic market segmentation model. The strategic challenge is to select those segments upon which the company will focus its attention.

The product development team is most concerned with the needs analysis requirements that seek to gather the more specific information necessary to create the superior targeted solutions for specific target markets.

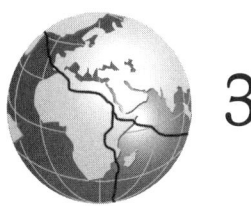

3

Strategic Opportunities and Responsibilities

When a project team is appointed to create a major new product or product line, it is usually endowed (albeit unwittingly) with a huge disadvantage. In the name of empowerment, participation, and teamwork, business theorists have quietly provided for one of the most unfortunate lapses in executive responsibility. That is, executives may unintentionally abdicate their most important job. Empowering employees does not mean giving up the key responsibilities of the executive, and the most important responsibility is the challenge of corporate strategy.

When a development team is given a "blank sheet of paper," such as a no-constraints mandate to develop "the next generation of products" or some other such mission, the project group has just been invested with the seeds of failure. No organization operates without constraints (although some may act as if they do, often paying a fearful price). No one is in a better position to understand those constraints than executive management, whose job it is to see that the organization satisfies its responsibilities and does not exceed its capabilities. If the management team delegates or otherwise abdicates its *strategic* re-

> *Strategic management responsibilities cannot be delegated.*

sponsibility, then they may as well arrive late, leave early, and take a very long lunch. They have no real purpose.

Strategy and the Process of Competing

Much current business literature confuses "strategy development" with the process of planning. Often, planning is equated with strategy, and the word *strategy* is used synonymously with planning. Even *Merriam-Webster's Collegiate Dictionary* implies the terms are interchangeable. This is genuinely unfortunate, because the resulting muddle makes it difficult for most managers to sort out the logic of strategic thinking. *Planning* can be applied to the most mundane and insignificant of activities, for example, "We have a plan to refurbish the lunchroom."

For better or worse, plans are about paper. Useful certainly, and necessary, but it is entirely possible to plan everything and accomplish nothing. We've all heard the quip "paralysis by analysis," and many project teams have experienced executive managers who would "spend months planning the trip but never quite start the car." They like to plan, but when the time comes, they shrink from the attack.

Strategy, in contrast, is about action. It's about overcoming an adversary in some area of conflict; in fact, there must be an adversary for the principles to be applied. Strategy is implemented with the full expectation of a response by the adversary. Strategic activities are not independent of the competitive environment—the marketplace. Strategy, then, is used to guide an organization to success in a *competitive* environment.

Unlike situations of military conflict, the goal in the business arena is never to destroy the competitor. It is often actually illegal to do so. The objective in business is *always* to win the

> *Planning is to strategy as management is to leadership—confusingly similar in usage, but quite different in effect.*

customers. The competitor is often in the way, also attempting to win the customer; hence, the principles of strategy are those by which the contest is ultimately conducted. Your target market segments, your profitable potential customers, are the goal. The customer is always the prize. The winner will often be the one who makes fewer strategic mistakes.

Strategy—the adversarial kind, not the planning kind—is rich in principles and concepts that are universal to the process of succeeding in an environment of conflict.

The "weapons" or tools of the business conflict are essentially the four "Ps" offered by E. J. McCarthy in the early sixties. Price, place (distribution), product, and promotion (sales, advertising, and promotion are combined in this definition of promotion) define the primary tools of competition. Quality, speed, knowledge, service, cost, and design are also much discussed as strategic weapons today. They are, of course, but on closer examination one will see that each falls comfortably within one of McCarthy's four Ps. A case could be made for including strategic acquisition as another kind of weapon—and acquisition can be very powerful—but again, what one is acquiring is almost always one or more of the four Ps (i.e., desired products, capacity to make products, knowledge of products, markets, etc., or distribution access).

How adroitly managers develop and use these weapons or strategic resources to compete will determine their degree of success in a competitive market. The way in which these resources are deployed to grow and prosper is in fact business strategy. Strategic management is about identifying opportunities, selecting the best, and then skillfully exploiting them.

Although product is the focus of this book, it cannot be totally isolated from the price, distribution requirements, and promotional potential, insofar as development activities are

> *Strategic management is about identifying opportunities, selecting the appropriate ones, and then skillfully exploiting them.*

concerned. The physical product frequently determines the potential for the successful and powerful application of the other three.

When product is the dominant variable in the tools of competition (the primary opportunity for differentiation and/or advantage), then product development becomes the dominant consideration in the formulating strategy. It is essential to recognize that "product development" is not really about creating products; it is about competing in the marketplace. (See Figure 3-1.) Thus, as a general rule, strategy should drive product development activities. Product development is most effective when it is viewed as "applied strategy." Development of anything just for development's sake is a luxury and a waste of resources that no organization can really afford.

Strategic Activities

Because few executives see their role as passive, the argument that they should consciously extend their activities to specific areas that increase the overall performance of the company should not be much of a stretch. In any event, we're not advocating a huge departure from what many managers are undoubtedly trying to do at present. We *are* advocating some very specific activities that have the potential to stimulate huge improvements in the market performance of a company's products. Following are concrete suggestions for making the needed strategic activities successful. The activities are relatively straightforward.

- *Define the business.* If the nature of the business is either unstated or defined too broadly, a great deal of time and effort will be wasted with well-intentioned product ideas that do not fit the company and its resources. Although it may seem a simple matter to create such a definition, most people find it much more time-consuming and elusive than it appears. However long it may take, it is worth the effort.

If management does not define the business clearly, it may well find itself trying to compete in markets where it has no competitive advantage, no profit, no strengths, and no future.

Figure 3-1. Product definition and competition.

**What do we mean by a product,
and
how do we compete?**

Products, especially industrial and commercial products, are complex aggregations of technologies, parts, and other tangible elements, as well as a host of intangible elements that we generally call services. As the diagram indicates, we can think of a product as three sets of elements:

  a. The core cluster of tangible and intangible elements;
  b. A separate cluster of tangible elements we will call facilitating products; and
  c. A separate cluster of intangible elements we will call facilitating services.

The core of the product is the essence of the product that competitors and customers all recognize as necessary parts of the product. Every competitor includes these elements, and we do not (and cannot) differentiate ourselves from anyone else on these elements.

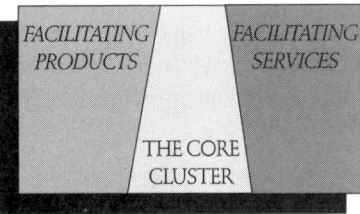

The facilitating products and facilitating services are ancillary items the presence and level of which are at our discretion. We differentiate ourselves from our competition using these elements. As products mature, and as market segments become smaller and smaller, the core increases in size as the notion of the product in the market segment becomes more complete; what were facilitating products and services become part of the core as everyone accepts them. More facilitating products and services need to be found.

Another trend has become evident. The importance of facilitating services has been increasing over time, and in many industries competition is now more on the basis of services than the product elements. Ask GM where its profits are derived; it isn't manufacturing.

A third trend is also developing; more of the facilitating products and services are provided elsewhere in the supply and distribution chains than from the facilities of the "manufacturer," the ostensible power in the chain. This makes it essential that the whole supply and distribution chain (sometimes called the company's value chain) be involved in strategic discussions and decisions—such as new product development decisions.

> *Product development is most effective when it is viewed as "applied strategy."*

○ *Choose the target markets.* By "target markets" here, we specifically mean target segments within the chosen "business." More precisely, these segments must be specific and narrow enough to be "operative," or usable by the product development group. Targets like "the prescription drug market," or "the classroom furniture market," or "the pressure washer market" are not nearly specific enough to ensure success. The key tool for target market selection is the strategic market segmentation model, introduced in Chapter 2 and discussed in detail in Chapter 4. A proper market segmentation model clearly describes the customer group (segment) in terms of *why* the people in this group buy *what* they buy.

If this kind of precision is not available at the outset, product development efforts will lack the kind of focus and clarity that guides the most successful product development activities.

○ *Choose the people.* It's not possible to create first-class products with second-class skills. Recruiting, hiring, training, developing, and retaining people with the knowledge and skill levels consistent with achieving corporate goals is a matter of strategic necessity. Retaining highly skilled development people is crucial. The challenges and limitations inherent in the culture of each individual company can make it impossible for even the most skilled new employee to succeed if he or she is hampered by lack of feel for the company. Chapter 5 discusses this topic at length, because it is difficult to find a more common reason for the failure of development projects. Employees who are both skillful and have an understanding of the organization are likely to be much more effective than those who lack such sensitivity.

○ *Provide the resources.* The "unfunded mandate" is the curse of all product development managers. The "unbudgeted project" is the curse of all financial executives. An unbudgeted project may cost as much or more than a budgeted one when all is said and done; it's just that no one had planned for it, and hence it can be extremely disruptive to everything else that was planned. When senior management is intimately involved in the product development activity, then it is both possible and reasonably painless to determine the "right" level of funding.

○ *Give ongoing support.* Ongoing support should not be confused with micro management. Be there when needed. Stay in touch. However, this is not just a casual level of support. When the attitude is one of truly being interested and wanting to be helpful, it can make a huge difference. Development projects frequently pose new and unfamiliar challenges. In such cases, management mentoring of the team or project leader can make all the difference.

Development projects frequently create opportunities or challenges beyond the experience of the group directly involved. If senior management is too distant, or unapproachable, but at the same time the only source of resolution, the opportunity may go unattended, or the challenge ignored until too late.

○ *Develop and communicate the new product screening criteria.* The "new product decision screen" is an important management tool (see Chapter 6). It is the best vehicle for defining the corporate criteria for a successful product to guide the rest of the organization. Once created, it will only occasionally need alteration, and it will save all that time currently devoted to deciding new product issues over, and over, and over again. The screen permits management to decide once, and then it can implement that decision frequently and easily.

When to Develop a Strategic Plan

There are companies with sales in the $400–$500 million annual sales range that do not have a structured, written strategic planning process. A company this size is far too large to be run on a cocktail napkin. Every company needs a plan to guide it. Only the very smallest cottage industry organizations can continue to prosper without committing the plan to writing (and nearly all of *them* would benefit from the exercise). The strategic plan is how focus is achieved and maintained in the face of relentless day-to-day responsibilities.

The length and complexity of the plan may vary with the size and scope of the organization. But longer is not better. This is not the place to include research findings, background material, or diverse points of view. The strategic plan is simply a concise statement of direction accompanied by key information about those primary elements that drive the company.

A sample format for a strategic plan is included in Appendix II. This format is only about seventeen pages long. If management executives cannot outline where they're going in thirteen pages, then they haven't yet learned to focus on the important and avoid the superfluous.

Product Development Strategies in a Global Marketplace

Not many years ago, discussion of the global implications would have been of direct interest to a relatively small number of U.S. manufacturers. In the past two decades it has become a matter of central concern for virtually all U.S. manufacturers. The key reasons are simple:

- To successfully compete in export markets it is necessary to understand both the needs of those markets and ways of successfully competing with local manufacturers in those markets.
- To successfully compete in domestic markets it is necessary to understand both domestic customers and foreign manufacturers and their products available in the United States.
- U.S. manufacturers now compete with the multinational located in Frankfurt, the small producer of parts in Taipei,

> *Strategic plans should be focused and concise. If it takes too many pages to say what's necessary, then something is wrong.*

> *It makes a difference:*
>
> *Alice, being lost, inquired of the Cheshire Cat, "Would you tell me, please, which way I ought to walk from here?"*
>
> *"That depends a good deal on where you want to get to," said the Cat.*
>
> *"I don't much care where—" said Alice.*
>
> *"Then it doesn't really matter which way you walk," said the Cat.*
>
> *"—so long as I get somewhere," Alice added as an explanation.*
>
> *"Oh, you're sure to do that," said the Cat, "if only you walk long enough."*
>
> Alice's Adventures in Wonderland
Lewis Carroll, 1865

   the machine efficiencies designed in Tokyo, and the offshore plant of the competitor down the street.
 ○ A single product may include engineering expertise from India, design expertise from Germany, marketing input from the United States, and product assembly economies in Mexico. In short, the need for a comprehensive command of strategic principles has never been greater.

It is no longer effective or efficient to develop products for introduction in the United States, test market them in the United States, and later simply introduce them to export markets by sending the drawings to international plants around the world. There may have been a time when such an approach was possible (though it may not have been ideal then either), but instant information access and global competition in virtually every industry has made such a strategy extremely hazardous today. Designing a product for U.S. or North American market segments only, then reengineering and redesigning the product for each successive market as it presents itself, is far too expensive to be considered seriously.

Those companies choosing to use product development as a strategic weapon have a range of choices. Each can be highly successful when used appropriately and with skill. Strategy development is a very powerful activity. Devising appropriate strategy poses several requirements for practitioners. It is one of the most important decisions a company will make and thus deserves considerable study and skill on the part of management. Strategic proficiency, at a minimum, requires:

- Working knowledge of strategy principles and alternatives
- Ability to stay focused upon the opportunity
- Performance goals
- Objective appraisal of the company's current or historical strategies
- Accurate competitive situation analysis
- Knowledge of key competitors and their leaders
- Objective appraisal of corporate resources
- Understanding of the "corporate will"

Specific Strategies

For the purposes here generic product strategies can be reduced to four. Each has strengths and weaknesses. Each can be employed with seemingly infinite variation.

1. Defend
2. Attack
3. Follow (imitate)
4. Hide (avoid direct competition whenever possible)

As with military strategy, it makes a difference who you are and where you are when you select a strategy. There are fundamentally two kinds of variables: those you control (skill, efficiency, determination, strategy, etc.) and those you don't (economic conditions, new technologies, health of customer's business, etc.). Let's examine each of these four strategies in the context of new product development.

Defend

Defensive strategies are inherently quite powerful forms (e.g., a $1,000 defense is generally considerably more effective than a $1,000 attack). It is simply the nature of the defensive position: A good defense can be extremely difficult to penetrate. On the downside, one cannot make relative gains using defensive strategies. Short of one's competitors destroying themselves, or their market effectiveness, one must attack; one must take offensive action.

"Market leaders" are the dominant companies in a particular market or segment. They are seldom dominant in every product segment in which they compete. They are typically the largest and most successful in the product market in which they are the leader. The leader has the largest market share. The leader may well be the product innovator, but its source of innovation may also emanate from skill at promotion, distribution management, or pricing. Leaders are invested with somewhat distinctive strategic demands in those markets they lead in.

The market leader, more than any other competitor, is concerned with defense (or preemptive offense) and often finds itself defending in multiple product markets simultaneously. The leader must defend against all contenders to protect each leadership position. Complacency may be as much an enemy as any market challenger. Some notable examples of market leaders that have successfully maintained their superior position against all comers for an extended period are Caterpillar, Procter & Gamble, and Microsoft.

There are many more examples of leaders who lost their position to one or more challengers, not infrequently through

> *Defense is inherently the stronger form of strategy.* —Napoléon Bonaparte

faulty strategies. Leaders may indeed possess unique strengths that can be *extremely difficult* for challengers to overcome so long as their defenses are skillfully constructed and competently managed. The primary defenses available are:

- The preemptive defense (attack them before they attack you)
- Control of distribution channels
- Copyright and patent protection
- Counter every challenge
- Develop and maintain a close customer relationship
- Promotional efforts

It is beneficial for every company to understand the primary defensive strategies, even if it is an attacker.

Attack

Market share is gained through one of the various attack strategies. Attack involves a direct, concerted action intended to improve the attacker's relative position. Whenever a company seeks an account, customer, or type of business that is currently served by another supplier, then some form of offensive strategy will be required to achieve that end.

At the tactical level the simple cold call on a potential new customer is the most basic form of attack. The current supplier is compelled to defend, usually by countering the attacker's sales pitch, product, price offer, or whatever. Thus begins a series of give-and-take we known as competition. If attackers understand the customers and their needs, they are able to focus their approaches on the precise area (features, benefits, price, durability, quality, service, etc.) that is most likely to effect a change to a new supplier. In the strategic sense the attacker has "focused sufficient resources at the decisive point to ensure success."

In mounting a defense, the current supplier usually counters the new offer. This may well set off a whole series of give-and-take, which may extend over months or even years. The ultimate winner will be the one able to offer the customer that combination representing the best value according to the customer's definition.

Leaders, followers, and "nichers" can all become "challengers" in the product markets of their competitors. Many, if not most, large companies compete in numerous product markets, and even the huge and successful Procter & Gamble is not the leader in all the markets it competes in. Challengers have numerous specific strategies available, several of which center on the product. The primary attack strategies are the following:

- Price discount
- Cheaper goods
- Prestige goods
- Product proliferation
- Product innovation
- Improved services
- Distribution innovation
- Manufacturing cost reduction
- Intensive promotion

You should never attack just to fight; you should always attack to win something. Success is determined by whether or not that "something" was won. Attacking without the clear intention to win something specific is merely to waste valuable resources. If you don't know precisely what you intend to win, then it's probably better not to attack at all. Nothing will be gained, of course, but nothing will be wasted either.

Follow

Numerous companies have become successful through a basic "follower," or imitator, strategy. By tucking in behind a leader, preferably one who is running at capacity or is otherwise complacent, a competitor can frequently reap the benefits of this abundance with "me too" products. Product development costs are obviously much reduced, and often the follower can use the same distribution channels. Such opportunities are generally transitory, however. They seldom last more than a few years, at which time the follower may have to abruptly change approach or risk disaster.

Followers or imitators often can find a rather comfortable market position by riding along just behind the market leader but always pulling up short of an open challenge to the leader's position (which might provoke a painful response from the leader). Some companies find this to be a very profitable position to occupy.

The danger to the leader is that these seemingly benign followers or imitators can quickly become challengers if they sense an opportunity (weakness) on the part of the leader. An undefended market may well be a greater temptation than the heretofore quiet follower can resist. To displace the leader, however, the follower must now adopt a different strategy: the strategy of attack. Some followers cannot adjust to these new strategic needs and try to displace a leader with a follower strategy. It doesn't work. The situation can be likened to that of the follower in the tactic of "drafting" in NASCAR racing. It only works when the follower stays tucked in tight behind the leader. Once the follower pulls out to pass, the requirements (and horsepower) change dramatically, and the follower now needs a different strategy.

Four general follower strategies can be used to execute a follower position:

- The counterfeiter
- The cloner
- The imitator
- The adapter

There is, of course, the danger that the competitor a company chooses to follow is, in fact, *not* doing the right thing. By follow-

> *Follower strategies work only so long as there is a leader to follow and the product lends itself to imitation.*

ing blindly, the follower may be copying the competitor's mistakes as well as its successes.

Hide

"Guerrilla" and "nicher" strategies are preferred by the smallest competitors. By consciously choosing not to draw attention to themselves, guerrillas can often reap benefits that would not be possible for larger, more visible organizations, which would tend to draw more competitive response. (See Figure 3-2.) When the big competition begin meddling in the nicher's market, the nicher can be hurt badly, and the large competitor may never even know it. "When the elephants dance, the ants can get crushed."

Figure 3-2. When elephants dance, ants get crushed.

Nichers seek to occupy a small but profitable segment—and to do so well enough as to not attract the attention of the market leader or other more powerful competitors. Nicher strategies are geared to reinforcing their unique form of specialization. Nichers have numerous strategic alternatives:

- The end-user specialist
- The vertical-level specialist
- The customer-size specialist
- The specific customer specialist
- The geographic specialist
- The product or product line specialist
- The product feature specialist
- The job-shop specialist
- The quality-price specialist
- The service specialist
- The channel specialist
- The technology-enhancer specialist

Nichers are always susceptible to the moves (intentional or otherwise) of larger competitors into their niche. The profitable niche can be spoiled by a fumbled incursion by a competitor, which may then exit the niche in search of greener pastures. The nicher may be irrevocably changed by the experience, and the niche may no longer exist in its previously attractive form.

Strategies for Growth, Maturity, and Decline

It makes a difference whether your company is competing in a growing, stable, or declining market. Such market conditions are generally beyond the individual company's control. These three situations are illustrated in Figure 3-3.

- *A Growing Market: Curve A.* Many competitors are lulled into complacence by the relative ease of growing. This is the most forgiving of all market situations. Competition is almost always less intense than in the situations that follow. Curve B is a bit more problematical. Growth is greater than inflation but

Figure 3-3. Growth, maturity, and decline.

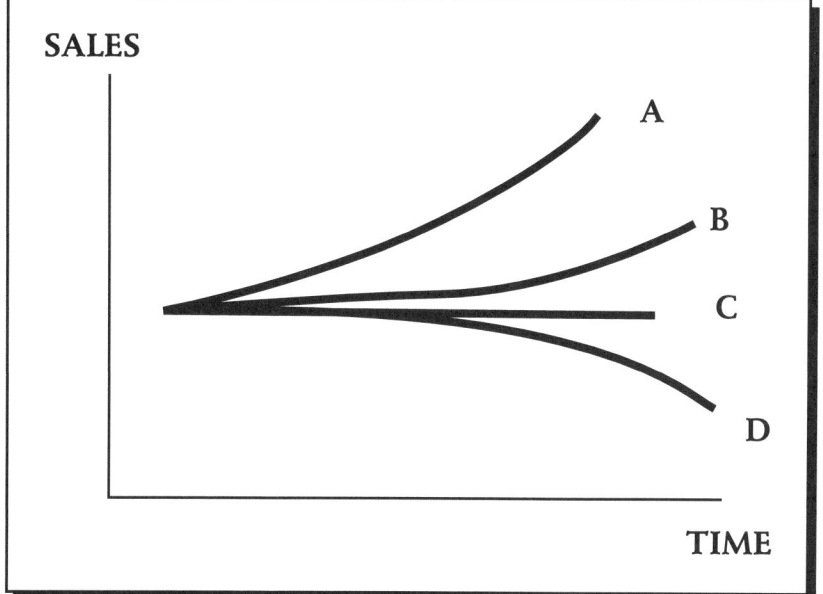

may not be sufficient to meet targets. When B follows a period resembling the very rapid growth of A, it is a warning sign that a fundamental change in strategy may be called for.

○ *A Stable or Mature Market: Curve C.* Growth may be limited to about the level of inflation, so any real growth one company is to enjoy will have to be taken at the expense of another. According to K. R. Harrigan of Columbia University, more than two thirds of all industries in the U.S., Japan, and western Europe are mature. Competition can range from gentlemanly to ruthless, and the fruits of product innovation can be enormous.

○ *A Declining Market: Curve D.* The market is in an advanced state of maturity. Some competitors are in the process of being driven out of the market. Most will not exit willingly, and every sales dollar will be contested fiercely. Endgame strategies require special attention.

With all these choices, and even infinite variations on the general themes, it is easy to see how so many companies can muddle their strategic choices.

Summary

We have made the case that corporate strategy is an executive-level responsibility, if for no other reason than no one else has the global picture in clear view. It cannot be performed effectively at lower levels. For all practical purposes, the weapons of strategy are the four Ps of product, promotion, price, and place (distribution).

There are four generic strategies available to any company: You can *attack* to gain customers or volume. *Defending* will never gain additional customers, but may be necessary to preserve what you have. A well-defended position is very strong. You can *follow* a leader and mimic their product and service offerings. Finally, the smaller company may find it very profitable to employ the guerrilla tactic of *hiding*, and enjoy considerable success out of sight of the larger and more powerful competitors.

Successful strategies are determined by market conditions, your position relative to competitors, and the resources you can bring to bear. Strategy is the art of winning, and as such is worth as much time as necessary to do it well.

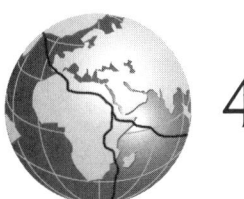

4

A Strategic Understanding of Customer Needs

Some years ago, one of the authors and his wife invited another couple to dinner. We had only met casually, but it seemed we might have interests in common, so inviting him and his wife to dinner seemed a good way to get to know each other.

Being interested in travel, food, and wine, my wife and I set to planning a dining experience for our new guests and soon-to-be friends. We figured that if we didn't stray too far from commonly available foods, yet applied our culinary skills in the most prodigious manner, we would produce a meal that would send our guests into ecstasy. We enjoy this kind of challenge, so we finally settled on the following menu:

- Assorted hors d'oeuvres, served in the living room with a special California champagne
- A first course of broiled sweet pepper salad with vinaigrette served with a Chassagne Montrachet white burgundy
- Grilled lambchops with rosemary with a Chateau Cos d'Estrounel red bordeaux
- Sautéed green beans with bacon and garlic
- Potato-turnip puree

- A small cheese course in the French style
- For dessert, a Grand Marnier soufflé and freshly ground gourmet coffee
- To top off the meal, a delicious twenty-year-old Neiport Porto

How could such a meal fail to delight even the most jaded of diners? We excitedly began preparation of the dining experience. The guests arrived.

After the initial greetings, we adjourned to the living room with a roaring fire to ward off the chill of winter. We popped the champagne and served the hors d'oeuvres. Our guests declined the champagne and somewhat sheepishly explained they didn't drink alcohol, asking for any soft drink instead. We don't drink soft drinks. So, ice water it was. An inauspicious beginning.

Needless to say, hors d'oeuvres and ice water are nothing to set the gourmand's heart to throbbing. Our guests, being vegetarians, also passed on the carefully prepared crab toasts. My wife and I looked at each other, and we could see the remainder of the evening going downhill fast.

In short, our guests had a wonderful evening of raw carrots, pepper salad, and pureed potatoes—all washed down with more ice water, of course, because they did not drink caffeinated beverages either.

It was a very, very long evening. We all had a dreary and embarrassing time. They acknowledged they probably should have mentioned their preferences but didn't think it would be a big deal, as generally there is always something for them to eat without inconveniencing others too much. After apologies all around, we parted graciously, never to see each other again.

How could we have been so stupid? A fair question, but after years of working in new product development, we know that we are not alone. Companies often fail to clearly identify likely customers and learn how to make them happy *before*

Assumptions can be truly dangerous.

spending money developing products, just as we failed to understand our potential new friends.

Understanding the Customer

Understanding the needs of the customer is an axiom found in all product development literature. So, how difficult can that be? We just put together a group to determine what we want to know for the project and survey a representative group of customers; maybe we go out and visit a few personally. Standard marketing practice, right?

Well, maybe—sometimes. In cases where there are millions of customers who obtain and use the product or service rather directly (e.g., some consumer goods), the survey methodology works about as well as any other. The results are subject to the normal hazards of survey and analysis practice, but there are few alternatives to reaching such an enormous number of contacts.

Other product markets, particularly industrial product markets (those wherein one business sells principally to another business or organization), pose a very different situation. Frequently, the person who uses the product is not the same person who purchases it. Large purchases may be made by a group or committee from different disciplines. The product may pass through several channels of distribution, each of which has its own needs that must be satisfied if the product is to ever find its way to the end customer. The client company may make use of "expert advisers" if the product or application is highly technical. The expert may not even be an employee of the client company. In such cases, which are common, the traditional survey method of "understanding customer needs" can be complicated beyond all reason. The survey method breaks down.

Undaunted, though, those determined to survey go out

> *Just because it's complicated doesn't mean it isn't worth figuring out.*

each day and study one or more groups, only to learn later that they have only partial information or even useless information. Making things worse, properly conducted surveys are costly to perform.

Making matters even more worse, the survey approach may require surveying eight or nine different groups. Because each group is different, or may play a different role in the purchase and use cycle, each survey has to be developed separately. The problem then becomes *how* to combine the disparate data from different questionnaires into a single clear and accurate picture of the marketplace (i.e., clean segments).

Most often, usually because of cost constraints, the company will make do with a single survey and develop the model from that data. The result is a little like opening an auto repair shop with one size screwdriver, one size wrench, and one hammer—there will be a lot of cases where the available "tool" does not fit the need!

Just Who Is the Customer, Anyway?

A couple of years ago, the authors spoke with the chairman of a large manufacturer of office furniture. When asked how the company determined whom to focus its efforts on, the chairman said matter-of-factly, "Our customer is the dealer. We really have no contact with or information about the end user." The company was disappointed that its efforts to expand to new sectors of the office furniture market had been less successful than planned. Senior executives were quite perplexed that their previous success was not simply transferred to the new target market. The problem was that they consistently oversimplified the diversity inherent in the various sectors of their marketplace. Pretend-

> *Traditional marketing tools for segmenting come up short in the business-to-business arena.*

ing the problem was more simple than it was seemed somehow preferable to dealing with the actual complexity in a methodical and calculated way. They preferred the simple answer, even if it was wrong.

Office furniture sounds like a rather straightforward product group. Most people don't think much about it at all; even those who work in offices every day. It is, however, representative of the complexity confronting the majority of business-to-business manufacturers. The sale of contract office furniture can easily involve all of the following players:

- An independent sales representative
- A product wholesaler
- An interior design firm
- An architectural firm if there is a new building or major renovation
- An office furniture dealer (retailer)
- An independent furniture installer
- A customer purchasing agent
- A department manager
- The actual user of the item

So, just which one *is* the customer? The answer is any—and all—of them, depending on the specific product and target market in question. None of the larger office furniture companies can continue to grow indefinitely with an obsessive focus on only one of these influence groups. The largest manufacturers in this industry clearly need to understand them all. Focusing only on the dealer, when there may be as many as eight other distinct participants in the sale, leaves innumerable opportunities for getting it wrong. This is a high price to pay for the comfort of simplicity.

The preceding example is in no respect unrealistic. Nearly all producers of business-to-business products face a similar (although maybe somewhat shorter) list of participants in a suc-

> *The complexity of business-to-business markets should not be underestimated.*

> *How can we expect to find any clarity or achieve focus if we can't even agree on who the customer is?*

cessful sale. Unfortunately, standard marketing tools were developed with a disproportionate emphasis on consumer products, which have a much more direct path to the end user. These tools often do not work very well when applied to industrial product situations. For that matter, many commonly marketed consumer products are composed of parts, subassemblies, or services that are outsourced by the ultimate manufacturer and thus not well served by the commonly available marketing tools either. Nearly everything sold to the ultimate manufacturer of a *consumer or industrial product* is a *business to business sale*, and offers the same challenges.

It is easy to see how the survey vehicle is at a great disadvantage for studying such a diverse and large group of participants. A company could spend $100,000 or more for a survey and learn only a small fraction of the information required to understand what is going on. To try to effectively segment such a complex market by survey methodology is unlikely to ever be satisfactory (although some research firms can produce really cute segment names). Unfortunately, most companies learn this the hard way.

Survey techniques are not without value. When the purpose of the information search is very specific, and when the subject audience is rather narrow and can be identified clearly, surveys can be useful. But as a primary tool for the industrial products manufacturer, the applications are decidedly limited.

A Better Way to Segment Markets

What is needed is a better method of segmenting markets, particularly for those business-to-business situations where there are multiple layers of participants. Fortunately, there *is* a better way to understand and segment markets: "interactive experience group conferencing."

The interactive experience group conferencing methodology uses experienced people (typically in-house folks) from sales, marketing, and sometimes customer service or others who have direct customer experience. Sales and marketing people are most commonly the ones who have a lot of direct experience trying to understand customers and their behavior. In facilitating numerous sessions of this type, we are nearly always impressed by the depth of knowledge available in any given company (and which the company is generally unaware of). In each case what was lacking was a methodical approach to obtaining the right information and then processing it into a workable segmentation model.

The critical difference between interactive experience group conferencing and just turning loose sales or marketing folks to "segment our markets" is the structured, repeatable process of the former, which invariably leads to effective segments. It is interesting to note also that the conferencing method works equally well in other countries, even those lacking demographic

> *"Interactive experience group conferencing" is a process that utilizes the experience of a group (usually seven to ten participants) whose members have direct and preferably broad customer experience in the various sectors of a given marketplace. They are guided by a trained facilitator to identify and document the key aspects of each of the different customer segments within the defined marketplace. Most companies have people in the organization with the information necessary to accurately segment markets, but lack the methodology to make it a reality.*

data, published government statistics, or directories accurate enough to even conduct a survey. Cultural differences are no obstacle, because the information is obtained from knowledgeable people from the same culture, obviating misunderstandings on that score. The method works because it does not depend on "data" that are seldom available, but rather upon people with knowledge. People with knowledge are almost always available, regardless of how primitive the country may be.

Capturing Subtle Differences

Often, the forces that really influence purchases are not at all obvious. It is of the utmost significance that our model captures the underlying reasons that determine customer behavior. Fly fishermen among us may appreciate the following example:

Fly fishermen are a rather specific group within the larger universe of fishermen. Unlike the bait fisherman, or those choosing spinning-type equipment, the fly fisherman is more than a simple fish hunter. Many would consider fly fishing to be the pinnacle of an arcane art. Their most frequent (but by no means only) prey is the trout.

Fly fishing equipment has changed relatively little in the past seventy or so years, with one notable exception: the fly rod. Up until shortly after World War II, fly rods were made of split bamboo (which is actually a member of the grass family). There has always been a technical interest within the fly fishing community, but after the war, fiberglass became a viable material for constructing fly rods (and is still used today to some degree). In the late fifties and throughout the next couple decades, the fiberglass rod nearly replaced the bamboo for the average fly fisherman. Sometime in the late seventies or early eighties, technology permitted constructing rods of carbon fiber, more commonly known as "graphite." The technologist would have us believe, with the use of charts, data, graphs, and empirical tests, that the graphite rod is a major advancement over the old bamboo rod.

If one does not look too closely, one would conclude that technology has won out for reasons of better performance . . . a clear victory for modern technology. But lo and behold, when one looks closely, one finds that the finest and most costly—and most treasured fly rods—are NOT the new and improved graphite rods. Indeed, the most prized rods are—you guessed it—handmade rods of split bamboo! A really fine graphite rod can be had at this writing for less than $600. But a fine split bamboo rod can easily cost $1,600–$2,000, and the best makers are backlogged for up to two years. Obviously, there is something going on here that goes considerably beyond pure engineering-performance specs.

Indeed there is. To limit one's concern to cost/performance ratio, the graphite rod would probably win hands down. But the soft glow of the golden bamboo, the flawless varnish, the figured wood reel seat, and the unique "action" of the finest bamboo rods have developed a coterie of followers who will pay several times the price of a "plastic" rod, and do so willingly—even eagerly. If we were in the fly rod business it would behoove us to develop some sort of "model" that would help us to understand the subtleties of why this would be so.

The Strategic Market Segmentation Model

Executives who see their customer reservoir as "the broad mass middle market for widgets" or some similarly "novel" generalization have placed themselves at a major strategic disadvantage before the competition for sales dollars has even begun. They suffer from a form of corporate myopia. Like a nearsighted marksman without his glasses, they are always aiming at a target they can never see clearly. Hence, they seldom get it quite

> *The idea of broad mass middle markets is pure fiction. All broad markets are composed of numerous smaller, narrow markets—sometimes many more than one would think.*

right. The occasional "bull's-eye" is more often due to chance than to skill.

It's not hard to find companies with this deficiency. Look at any of the companies that see themselves as experts in delivering low-cost, high-value mass merchandise ("economy" or "budget" products). They aren't hard to find. Their products often look like they were designed by the manufacturing engineers without benefit of any customer input—generally because they were! Such companies often have truly enviable cost structures. One only marvels at what they could do if they just knew a little about the people who buy their products. Usually they do not, unfortunately. These are often the companies that state, "The distributor or dealer is our customer," as if that explains anything or excuses their ill-designed products.

Other executives see the market as one huge reservoir of opportunities where leadership is demonstrated by the courage to reach out and grasp opportunities "as they come along." This buccaneer style of leadership may occasionally succeed also; it looks particularly attractive vis-à-vis *inactive* management of any kind. The problem here is that this swashbuckling approach of taking opportunity as it comes is really the *absence* of a strategy. Because the selection of customers and markets is governed by circumstance (what comes along) rather than choice, the product mix is often "schizophrenic" and thus more difficult and costly to market.

Such opportunistic product choices also offer little opportunity for common platforms from which to manufacture efficiently and little leveraging of specific corporate skills, facilities, distribution, or investment. In the haste to "never pass up an order," the company usually finds itself at some later point with a lot of products it wishes it did not have.

> *Not all management groups will see the light—even though any close study of the marketplace would provide ample evidence.*

Some of these companies may find the strategic approach very difficult. Management may be unable to see things any other way. An obsession with beating down the cost of me-too products, taking every order, or competing with continuous price cutting can operate to the exclusion of all else. Ultimately, they will fail. Or, worse yet in some ways, the company will be condemned to a market purgatory where there is no customer loyalty, no personal satisfaction, no profit, and no future.

To avoid such pitfalls, you first need to determine how to effectively segment markets. Basically, there are four dimensions by which markets can be divided:

1. *Product Type.* Easy to do because you can easily get numbers on how many are sold. The trouble is that it tells you almost *nothing* of any value about the customer.
2. *Customer Type.* Very common. Demographic information is usually available (company size, company type, income, age, gender, etc.). Better than product type but still fails to provide enough insight for much precision.
3. *Functional Needs of Customer Group.* Generally the most useful but also the most difficult information to obtain and convert into usable segments.
4. *Geographic Location.* Sometimes useful for some product types.

Because nearly all products are materially affected by more than one variable, possibly all four, the ideal segmentation methodology will encompass all four approaches.

We use the "scientific method" to create the strategic market segmentation model. That is, we carefully develop a hypothesis (our tentative segmentation model), then we validate that hypothesis in the marketplace. Using the scientific method has several genuine advantages. First, it is a very efficient method. Developing the hypothesis usually requires only a few days. Validation takes a bit longer but overall is quite cost-effective. Second, it is effective. In combination with interactive experience group conferencing, the scientific method produces a detailed and multidimensional model that offers insights that are all but impossible to obtain by other methods. Third, risk of an inaccurate model is greatly reduced. Surveying is essentially a one-shot game, and with the hypothesis/validation approach we quickly detect any discrepancies. Because of the validation step, the model also tends to gain credibility within the organization more easily. Finally, the model is easily revised or updated without starting from scratch.

The strategic market segmentation model involves three distinct steps:

1. Developing the hypothetical model
   - Selecting the group participants
   - Scheduling the conference
   - Conducting the two-day session
   - Documenting the hypothetical model

2. Validating the hypothetical model
   - Selecting customers to interview
   - Developing the interview format
   - Conducting the validation interviews
   - Documenting any differences between hypothesis and the validation interviews

3. Revising and finalizing the model
   - Determining if changes are required
   - Finalizing the model

Developing the Hypothetical Model

First, we need to select the experience group conference participants. Normally, these participants come from the in-house marketing and sales departments. If these people are not available or for some reason not suitable, then carefully selected outside personnel can be drawn on instead. For example, in a case where a company uses independent manufacturer's representatives in lieu of an in-house sales force, carefully selected reps can provide the input. Dealer or retailer sales personnel have been used satisfactorily in instances where an in-house sales department was not available. The key is that the participants should have direct customer experience.

Experienced sales personnel are usually to be preferred. Marketing personnel with direct sales experience are also extremely valuable. The preferred experience for a conference group is as follows:

- Direct customer experience (usually sales)
- Diverse customer experience (types and sizes of customers)
- Intimate familiarity with the various influencers in the sales process

It's worth noting that some management groups unfairly undervalue the knowledge of their own salespeople. If sales are not currently soaring, it's common for them to form the opinion that the sales department is underperforming. It's only a step away to presume that if they're not meeting the sales goals, then they must not be sufficiently knowledgeable for something as important as strategic market segmentation. We can safely say that we've seldom found that to be the case. In any event, if a particular group is found wanting (and the facilitator should have no trouble seeing this), then it is relatively easy to conduct one or more additional sessions to ensure the input is complete and accurate.

Creating the Segment Model

The conference to develop the hypothetical model is usually a two-day affair. The first half-day is usually devoted to preparing the group for what will follow. This is primarily an interactive educational experience wherein the participants come to understand the purpose of the segmenting activity, its importance to

Underestimating the knowledge value of the sales force can be costly.

the company, how it will be used, and what they can expect over the next two days.

The remainder of the day is devoted to background material on segmenting markets and using the resulting model. The participants are usually the most experienced people available and should be brought into the process as important contributors. It is a severe error to bring them to headquarters, do a fast "brain drain," and then send them back to wherever they're from without their really knowing why they were brought to headquarters in the first place. Results are always superior if the participants are brought into the process as full and valued partners.

Development of the actual model takes place in a large room with plenty of whiteboard space. It involves a rather rigorous procedure, conducted by a trained and capable facilitator skilled at seeking specific information. To begin, one participant is asked to select a customer with which he or she is very familiar. The information development process then follows a detailed series of questions that follow the general pattern of the four market dimensions noted earlier—product type, customer type (demographic profile), functional needs, and geographical location. Once this particular customer has been explored in detail, a different person in the group is asked to select a customer from his or her personal experience that is different from the customer just explored. The process is then repeated.

The process continues as long as necessary to ensure that no one in the group can think of a single customer that is not represented by the categories listed on the board. Then, the various types shown on the board are carefully examined, and any "duplications" are merged. When this process is complete, the board will usually contain between eight and fifteen unique types. These types represent an intermediate step and are known as "broad product markets."

At this point we have some valuable distinctions between

The hypothesis development phase is no place for a "casual" approach.

A Strategic Understanding of Customer Needs

customer groups, but we do not yet have "segments" (also sometimes called "narrow product markets"). "Segments" are very precisely defined as unique customer groups that are "homogeneous within each group and heterogeneous between groups. At this juncture, our groups are interesting, but they are not "clean" yet. Obtaining clean segments requires another rigorous effort.

Usually at the beginning of the second day, the group is started off with careful instruction on developing clean narrow product markets. Then, the attendees are divided into subgroups, each of which will take one or more broad market categories and, using a rigorous process, divide the broad product markets into hypothetical narrow product markets. When the group members are confident the narrow product markets are as close to perfect as they are able to get, the hypothesis development phase is complete. It is typically an exhausting but rewarding effort, and the group is always quite proud of what they have just created. We have our hypothetical market model. Now we need to verify the accuracy of the hypothesis.

Validating the Hypothesis

Validation is a critical step. Now that we have clear and carefully crafted definitions of our hypothetical segments, we need to make sure those in the segment are actually as we have portrayed them. The way to find out is to visit them at their location for an interview, which should take an hour or so. During this

> *Relentless pursuit of clarity and completeness is essential in a good facilitator.*

> *Participants are typically amazed at the accuracy of their model when they meet with customers.*

discussion, the interviewer seeks to discover whether this client indeed falls into the segment it is thought to. Once we have talked to a few who fit into our segment, we can feel pretty sure that it is a real segment.

Should any of the interviews produce a customer that does not fall into one of our previously identified segments, then we have a little more work to do. It's necessary to revisit the model and include the newly identified segment. Ordinarily, the original model is very close. In many cases, there are no additions or deletions at all.

When setting up the interviews with customers, it is inadvisable to be too candid about what you are doing. One does not want to mislead customers or potential customers, but it is sufficient to say that you are very interested in understanding them better and would like to know more about how and why they purchase what they purchase. It would not be appropriate, or productive, to arrive at a customer's office and explain your presence by saying that you're defining market segments and you want to make sure you have that customer properly identified as being in the "cheapskate" segment! Not all segment categories will be seen as complimentary by the customer described in them, so it's far more politically astute not to get into such technical specifics at all. Thank them profusely for their time, and present them with a small gift if you like, as a sign of appreciation for their sharing their time with you.

Once sufficient interviews have been conducted to leave you confident that your model is a good one, and that you don't know how you could improve on it, the validation phase is over. Two or three interviews in each segment may be all that is required to achieve a comfort level. If unsure, interview more customers. All that's left after the interviews are over is to document your visits so that any information needed for refinements to the model is accurate and available for reference.

Revising and Finalizing the Model

All that remains is to make the necessary changes, if any, to the written model. Once final, it should be written up in a professional manner and documented for future use. Write up the model and definitions with as much care as you would expect to find in a document of such importance to the company. You have just created a strategic corporate asset. The value of your model is much greater than the cost and time you have invested. The model should be treated as company confidential. Your view of the marketplace, which is used to guide your business strategy and your product development investment, is valuable. Why share it with your competitors? Let them figure the world out for themselves.

Summary

A structured and specific understanding of your chosen marketplace is the place to begin all corporate strategy. The selection of precisely whom your company will serve is arguably the most important decision management will make. When the target customer(s) is unclear, the business immediately starts to become inefficient. Nowhere is this more true than in product development, where highly specific decisions must be made as to what the product will do, how well it will do it, how much it will cost, and how it will be delivered. The more unclear the target, the more inefficient the product will be, as it seeks to do too much for too many with too little.

Traditional survey techniques are not best suited to segmenting markets, particularly industrial product markets. The interactive experience group conferencing methodology is far superior. The interactive experience group conferencing approach not only results in more accurate and useful segmentation, but is typically less expensive to create and maintain as well.

A company's view of the market (i.e., its segmentation model) is a valuable corporate asset, and should be regarded and maintained as one would any other valuable asset.

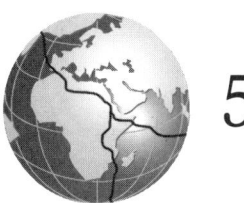

5

Product Development and Corporate Culture

The average company is a complex amalgam of individual values and personalities. The collective experiences and values make up what we commonly call the corporate culture, the shared values and beliefs that underlie a company's identity. It is different from its individual parts even though it cannot exist without its constituent parts. Corporate culture, and the corporate personality that emanates from the culture, permeates every aspect of an organization and provides the environment within which we attempt to develop products for the company. This environment can run the gamut from highly supportive to outright hostile.

One Size Does *Not* Fit All

Corporate culture is certainly a common reason that otherwise brilliant strategies fail miserably. Usually, when change is desired, it is because change is needed. When one seeks to change the product development process, it can usually be presumed that the existing system is not working as desired.

Understanding your corporate personality will allow you to better adapt the new product development process to the individual needs of the company. For most companies, the most pragmatic approach to the new product challenge is to first understand the nature of the corporate personality, then fit the product development process and new product strategies to the realities of the culture you have.

Although the *fundamentals* of a good product development process do not differ appreciably, there are several dimensions on which the process can and should be adjusted to achieve a good fit. Some of the key dimensions on which implementation of a new product development process can be varied are the following:

- Speed of implementation
- Level of complexity
- Degree of analysis undertaken
- Extensiveness of employee training
- Level of integration with corporate plan

All of these dimensions, and changes to them, are influenced by corporate culture. Thus, when we seek to implement any new or improved product development system, corporate culture becomes a matter of the greatest importance. Understanding the prevailing culture, and knowing how to work with it—or around it—is of central concern to the company. Change, any significant change, is always accompanied by a certain amount of organizational resistance, the objective of which is to return to a familiar, nonthreatening, and hence more comfortable situation. Improving or replacing the product development process is no exception.

The corporate personality or culture directly affects the following:

- Corporate management style
- Degree of risk taking or risk avoidance
- Level of market competitiveness

> *Successful product development goes hand in hand with an understanding of the predominant corporate culture.*

- Degree of focus and task achievement
- Sense of purpose and sense of urgency
- Value placed upon market performance
- Level of innovation that can reasonably be achieved
- Reward for success and penalty for failure

Every successful consultant learns early on that client companies have unique personalities. The most successful understand that their ability to successfully interpret the cultural characteristics of the client is key to getting results. The less successful consultants hammer their heads against the stone wall of theoretically correct solutions, which fail the test of "client fit." Even though a recommended course of action may be "technically" correct, there are often reasons unique to a particular client that cause the recommendation to be rejected outright or to be "accepted" but remain unimplemented.

The predominant cultural qualities of a company always affect the product development effort; they will be either a blessing or a curse, depending on the situation. A company that has emphasized risk avoidance for years and then suddenly encourages its employees to strive for great innovations to outperform competitors is probably going to be disappointed with the results. Such a strategy may seem totally rational to management. The people who will be doing the work, however, will find the past cultural pressure to "take no unnecessary risks" to be much stronger than the current call for innovative excellence. At the very least, it is unlikely to happen on the first try. Failure to recognize and make provisions for such cultural characteristics in any company invites failure.

Sources of Corporate Culture

A company's history goes far toward forming its personality. Many diverse factors go into any company's history, but there is

> *A company's culture is one of the most powerful influences on its ability* to compete.

little doubt that "where we come from" has a great deal to do with "who we are."

The Corporate Life Cycle

Ichak Adizes provides us with a model for examining a firm's past, present, and future.[1] He views corporate life cycles as a diagnostic tool. Adizes proposes several distinct stages (see Figure 5-1) in the life cycle of corporations and suggests that we can use knowledge of these stages to successfully explain corporate behavior and deduce specific remedies to problems. Although Adizes does not specifically address corporate culture, the behaviors described are highly instructive, and each implies a general cultural behavior set. Using Adizes methodology, we can glean some important implications for successful product development.

Briefly, the early stages (courtship, infant, and adolescent) are dominated by an entrepreneurial personality. The company is typically rather small and still driven by the personality of its founder.

To get to "prime," the company must make the often tempestuous transition from the freewheeling, deal-making entrepreneurial zest of the adolescent organization to one with more structure. At this point it must make the adjustment to the increased controls and formalized processes necessary to operate

Figure 5-1. Adizes's corporate life cycle.

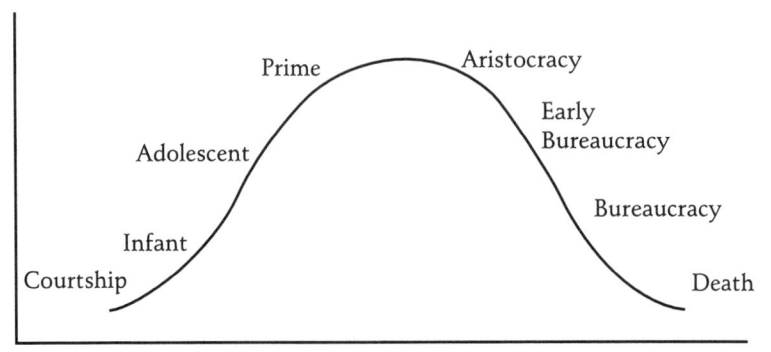

the larger and more encompassing organization. The "cowboy" management style gives way to the professional management of the corporation in prime.

Often, in the pre-prime stages, the founder of the company is also the driving engine behind the development of the company's products. The ideas, approvals, and financing decisions may all emanate from the boss. As the company grows, however, the requirements usually become too much for any single individual to manage—although the boss may try. At this point, the company is probably ready for the kind of development process proposed in this book. Most organizations will be well into the growth phase before they begin to recognize the inadequacies of their current processes (or on the downhill side of the curve desperately looking for a way back to the successes of prime).

In the mature or declining phases of an organization's evolution, the development situation is quite different. In contrast to little structure, the declining organization may well have deeply entrenched processes and vested interests that are actively protected by those who see themselves as being in charge of protecting the status quo. In the early phases, "processes" and "procedures" are seen (often rightly) as unnecessary encumbrances to fast development.

Implications from the Corporate Life Cycle Model

In the earliest stages, resources are probably the greatest constraint to strategic product development. In these stages, the ability to apply strategic principles to product development depends heavily upon the individual entrepreneur, and perhaps a very small coterie of engineers or designers. Processes are very informal and reflect the personalities of the individuals involved. Apple Computer started this way. In the early phases, Steve Woczniak and Steve Jobs *were* product development.

The growth phase is a real challenge for most companies. Things are going well, and growth is fast. The growth may or may not be sustainable under the current strategy, but the overriding philosophy is "don't rock the boat." It is very difficult to break into the frenetic culture of the firm in this phase.

Prime is a different animal altogether. To have achieved prime, the company has successfully instituted at least some of the processes and controls necessary to stabilize the organization and perpetuate its success. Organizations in prime find implementing strategic product development to be quite consistent with the changes they have already been implementing. Prime is, almost by definition, a healthy culture, and making the move to strategic product development is a logical extension of current events.

The mature organization may also find the move to strategic product development easy if it already realizes that things are slowing down and it needs to reverse course. Not all mature companies realize or understand the changes they are undergoing. The temptation is strong to just keep on going, continuing to enjoy past successes.

In the later life cycle phases, resistance to change may be very strong. In such cases, if the problem is not fully recognized, and the decision to change not fully accepted, then change will be difficult and very time-consuming. It can be done, but it requires strong leadership and extended commitment.

Although the corporate life cycle model is not the answer to all product development questions, it is very useful to know where a company lies on the curve and deduce the likely behavior. This can help in developing appropriate implementation plans.

Corporate Orientation

Another straightforward and useful tool is the corporate orientation model. Every company exhibits a distinctive cultural profile. Often this profile takes the form of a bias that may be either mild or strong in the direction of a particular "point of view." Usually such a bias stems from the historical successes of the company, which further strengthen the particular orientation that has worked in the past. The most commonly identified orientations, shown in Figure 5-2, are manufacturing/operations, technology, customer/market, vendor/supplier, and distribution. A company may find that it has a particular competence in a specific area and build on that strength.

Figure 5-2. Company orientation.

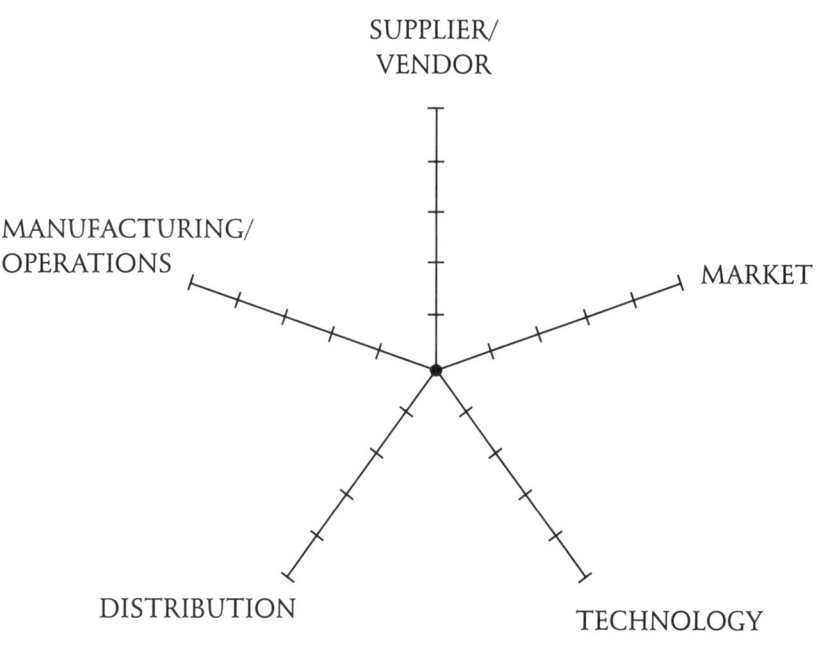

It is helpful to understand your company's orientation, because it will often prejudice decisions in one direction or another, often to the detriment of the development effort. It's a worthwhile exercise to examine your company and do a quick plot of your profile. It's a straightforward process that may be as informal as a single individual's plotting his or her view of the company or as complex as rating the company on each orientation by surveying or interviewing a wide number of employees.

When the results bend strongly in favor of a particular orientation, it can be said that the company has a "dominant orientation." In and of itself a dominant orientation is neither positive nor negative. A company may be justifiably proud of its achievements in a particular area, and these achievements may produce great benefits to the company. Typically, however, a strong bias in favor of even the most beneficial strength tends to suboptimize the potential for innovation in new products. It is a caution signal. It is essential to be aware of a dominant orientation and to always ask, "What am I missing here?" Figure 5-3 illustrates such a dominant orientation in the form of a bias toward the customer or market.

You may be asking, "Isn't it critical to be customer oriented?" Without a doubt, customer orientation is essential to the successful competitor, but weaknesses in the other areas are likely to cause problems. By its very nature, a dominant orientation represents a company that is out of balance. A company whose profile looks like that shown in Figure 5-3 may at first glance appear to have satisfied customers, but such is usually not the case. Given the extreme difficulty in achieving manufacturing effectiveness, cost control, and effective working relationships with suppliers and distributors, customers are unlikely to be satisfied at all.

Figure 5-4, in contrast, shows a more balanced or integrated company. The more integrated company will find it easier to innovate because it will be less fixated on the dominant orienta-

Figure 5-3. Dominant orientation.

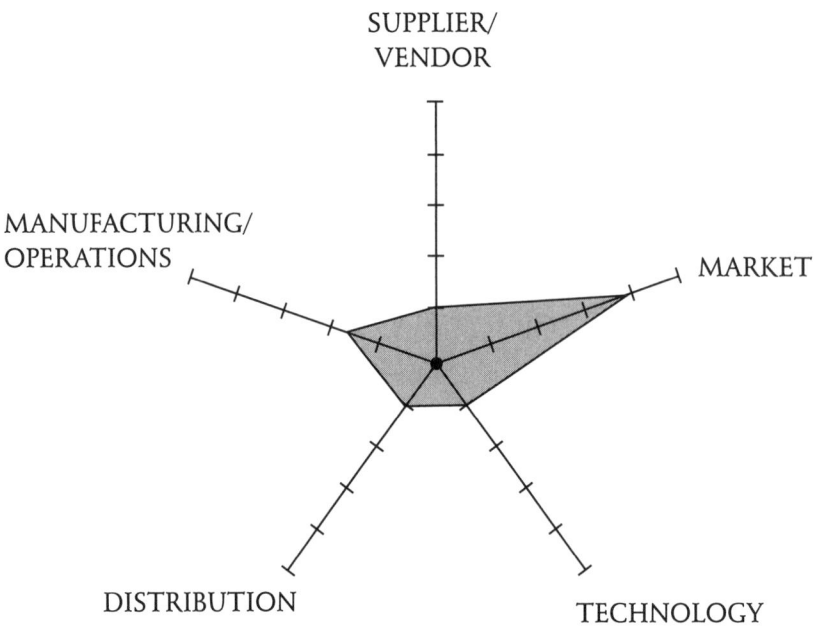

Figure 5-4. An integrated—or balanced—orientation.

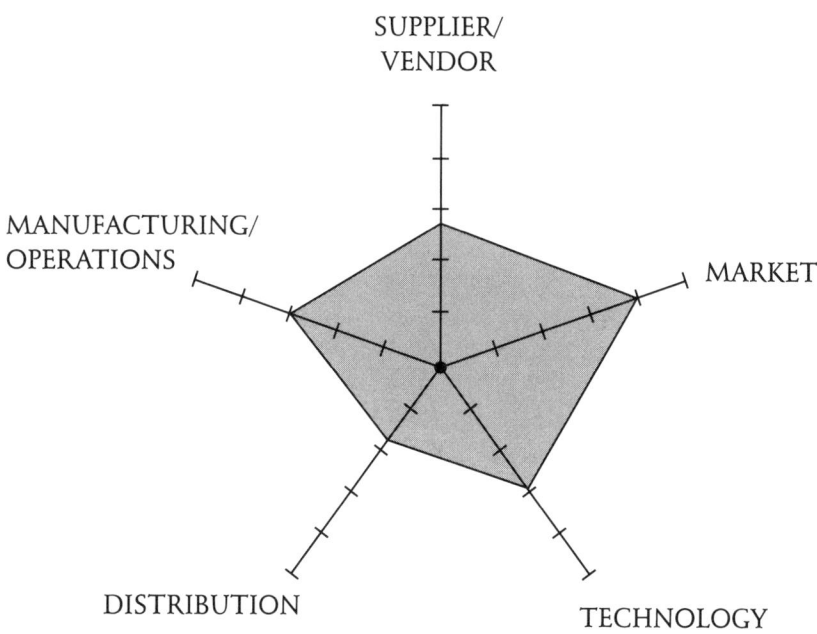

tion. The purpose of forming a multidisciplinary development team is to achieve just this kind of balance in the project. Any dominant orientation will generally work against balancing the inputs to the development project.

Other Factors Shaping Corporate Culture

The personality of any company is shaped by a combination of both internal and external factors. There are four primary influences, however, that in conjunction effect a unique corporate culture: values, a competitive imperative, company history, and leadership style (see Figure 5-5). There are also various "depths" at which cultural influences operate, and you need to bear them in mind as you think about managing change (specifically product development).

Values

The values of a strong leader, particularly in the early life cycle phases, tend to permeate the organization. The values of the entrepreneur tend to be the values of the organization. If the entrepreneurial zeal of the owner stops at nothing to get an order, then the organization will adopt that behavior because it will result in reward and promotion.

If the leader is cautious, hesitant, and indecisive, then the organization will read clearly that leaping to the fore with initiative will be a dangerous way to behave. Those who show initiative will tend to make the cautious leader uncomfortable; hence, those promoted will tend to be more like the leader. They can then "keep an eye on" those with initiative, so these self-starters don't "get the company into mischief." The message will travel quickly that being cautious is the road to promotion.

Figure 5-5. Organizational culture.

INVISIBLE   **VISIBLE**

←——————————————————→

Shared Values:

Significant goals and interests that are shared by most of the people in a group, that serve to shape group behavior. Often these values will persist for an extended period even with changes in group memberships.

Group Behavior:

Common or pervasive ways of acting that are found in a group that persist because group members tend to behave in ways that teach these practices (as well as their shared values) to new members, rewarding those that fit in and sanctioning those that do not.

←——————————————————→

HARD TO CHANGE   **EASIER TO CHANGE**

Adapted from John P. Kotter and James L. Heskett, *Corporate Culture and Performance*, 1992.

Some values are negative and more detrimental to the development of new products than others. Aversion to innovation, change, reasonable risk, and competitiveness are the most inhibiting to the creation of new products. After all, new products are by their nature new and different and will generally require at least some change. A process that is too "value constrained" will seldom produce much in the way of real competitive advantage.

John P. Kotter and James L. Heskett[2] provide a useful view of the role of shared values and group behavior on organizational culture. An adaptation of their model, which includes a "visibility continuum," is shown in Figure 5-6.

Those factors that constitute the part of culture that is hardest to change are invisible. "Easier" to change does not mean "easy" to change, however, and changing behavior (the easiest to accomplish) does not imply permanent cultural change; remove the incentive for changing behavior, and it will cease.

A Competitive Imperative

A sense of urgency borne of necessity goes a long way in defining a healthy company's personality, at least in the growing phases.

Figure 5-6. Primary influences on corporate personality.

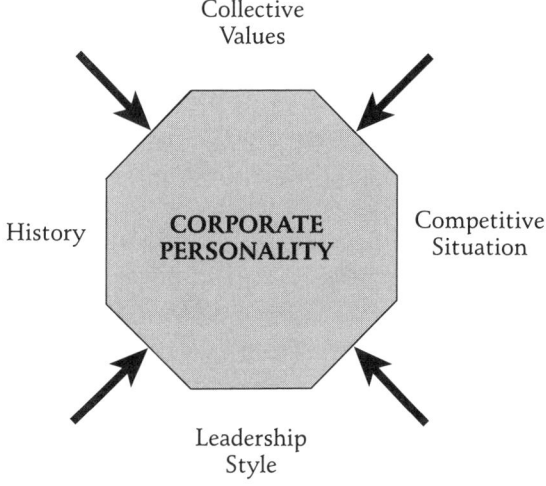

Companies in protected or heavily regulated industries may find that this legislated environment can contribute to the formation of a corporate personality that is different from that which evolves naturally in an environment of greater market freedom. Such organizations are also less likely to be aggressive, energetic, or innovative, because there is little incentive for taking chances.

A History of Success

Companies that have experienced great success and high profits are fertile ground for the germination of an unhealthy culture. It makes little difference whether the company has experienced this success because of visionary entrepreneurship or just entrepreneurial luck. Substantial success in any of the early phases of development is often the precursor of corporate overconfidence and arrogance as management attributes that success to its own brilliance. Such a history can herald an inward focus that can cause management and employees to undervalue customers and other contributors to their success.

Leadership Style

A fourth and possibly the most influential factor is the leadership style employed by management. There are a number of models and methods describing different styles of management. They are useful in diagnosing this key element in shaping a corporate personality. Figure 5-7 shows one classification scale of management characteristics; the individual manager's pattern of characteristics is that manager's style.

Obviously, the influence various leadership styles can have on the process of developing new products is tremendous. None of the dimensions is inherently good or bad per se. The total combination of characteristics is more significant, because strength in one area may compensate for weakness in another. Each dimension has its merits, but each also influences the environment for the creation of successful products. Success comes from knowing what your style is and its strengths and weak-

Figure 5-7. A diversity of management characteristics.

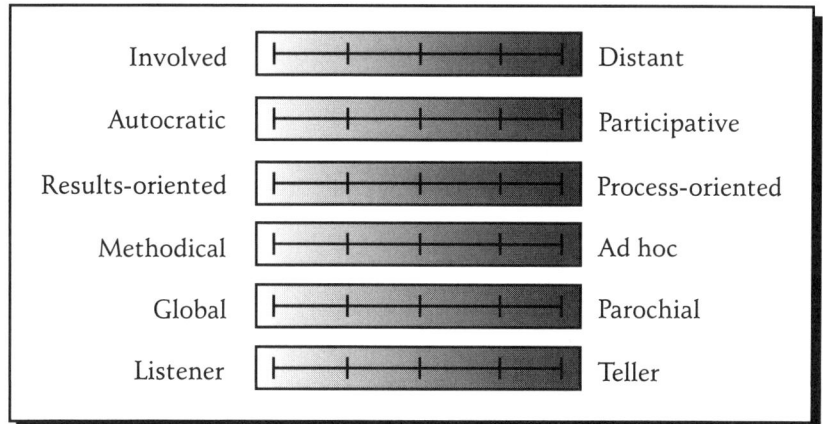

nesses, understanding how your style influences the results, and making modifications in behavior to achieve your goals.

Corporate Personality Types

To be able to put the idea of corporate personality to work in ways that will help product development efforts, we need to identify the major corporate personality "types." It is not necessary that the classification scheme be all-inclusive or perfect in every respect. It is necessary that it be representative and helpful in guiding the development process. You also need to always be aware of the strengths and limitations of each corporate personality type. If the new product efforts get too far from the expectations for a particular type, the team is usually in for rough sailing.

The model here divides personalities into six types.

○ *Entrepreneurs.* The entrepreneurial culture is often found in smaller organizations, always seeking new opportunity. Such an organization is less likely to fully exploit current products than it is to seek new ones. For the development effort, it usually offers a fair wind to new ideas and projects. Usually fast movers, entrepreneurs may want to go to market too quickly in the search for new opportunity. They are also prone to outstripping available development resources.

- *Technocrats.* Technocratic organizations like technology, process, and equipment opportunities. Any management style may be encountered, although too often the celebrated cause is that of cost reduction. Frequently, the technology takes over and runs roughshod over solid strategic and financial considerations. Such organizations may encounter great successes but will likely be erratic and find repetition of those victories difficult.
- *Economists.* Unlike the foregoing, the "bean counters" have the greatest influence in economist cultures. Often management is too cautious when the numbers are in question, as they often are in matters of innovation and new products or opportunities. Overambitious projects are likely to encounter this cautious streak early on in the project, and without convincing data the opportunity may go wanting.
- *Nobility.* The culture of nobility has usually had a history of great success, although it may have been years ago. A general feeling exists among management that the organization is "entitled" to future success, and hence executive members may feel that the hard work and innovation required of others is beneath them. The organization is quite susceptible to chronic complacency. Obviously, new product development can be very difficult if sufficient attention and funding is not directed to the effort.
- *Bureaucrats.* In bureaucratic cultures, process and procedure are highly valued. Often the development effort is saddled with voluminous books of procedures, most of which typically have more to do with following the rules than they do with supporting innovative and successful products. Procedure should always support and encourage *the desired result*. Red tape is not helpful to the development team in achieving its goals and is counterproductive. Bureaucrats may also have a long history of steady success, which may or may not have been hard earned. In any event, the constraints imposed by excessive bureaucracy can be deadly to new products.
- *Performers.* The performance-oriented culture, although it may be fast, furious, and unforgiving, is likely to be a fertile

environment for new product development. Because success is valued and management approaches risks in a mature and thoughtful manner, innovation is supported. Strategic decisions are not treated lightly, nor is the need to constantly remain ahead of the pack. The performer's history may be mixed, and some of the best performers have learned their lessons in the school of hard knocks. Management tends to be entrepreneurial in style and economic in its decision process. Procedure is neither seen as good nor bad, just prudent and necessary to keep the train on the rails. Too much control is avoided when possible.

Healthy and Unhealthy Cultures

Most readers' experience will confirm that there is a correlation between healthy corporate culture and superior long-term performance. Those who have done research on the subject also confirm this correlation. A company with a truly healthy culture seeks out ways to improve the product development process.

Companies with unhealthy cultures usually find it considerably more difficult to implement a strategic approach to product development. In these situations, ignoring the realities will almost certainly result in either poor return on the process investment or outright rejection by the organization. Unhealthy cultures have certain common components. Kotter and Heskett[3] identified three:

1. Managers tend to be arrogant.
2. The culture tends not to place high value on customers, stockholders, or employees.
3. These cultures tend to become hostile to leadership and other engines of change.

Summary

Again, strategy should always precede product development, and new products looking for an internal or external constituency should be by far the exception rather than the rule. Whenever possible, which is nearly always, the company should clearly know what it intends to do with the new products in the marketplace well before the projects are even funded.

Notes

1. Ichak Adizes, *Corporate Lifecycles: How and Why Corporations Grow and Die and What to Do About It* (Englewood Cliffs, N.J.: Prentice-Hall, 1988).
2. John P. Kotter and James L. Heskett, *Corporate Culture and Performance* (New York: The Free Press, 1992).
3. Ibid.

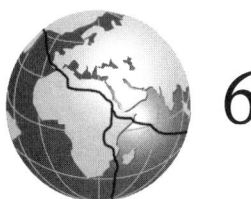

6

The New Product Decision Screen

In thousands of companies across the world today, a management group will assemble to discuss approving or nixing some new product project. In virtually every case there will be questions about progress, discussion of unsolved difficulties, and concern about whether the project will deliver the new product at or below budget. Few projects are probably "right on target" for all the performance criteria and cost projections; it is the nature of product development. Most groups will, at some point, launch into familiar discussions of whether the performance criteria can be modified downward, or whether they could pass along higher-than-expected costs to customers. What situation is "close enough" to approve proceeding with the project—or stopping it?

Consider the hypothetical company Axlerod Manufacturing. At Axlerod some of the most common development questions at management meetings are these:

- Are we going to be able to bring it in to sell at the target price?
- Are the development costs on budget?
- What are the technical problems yet to be solved?
- What is the proposed performance trade-off to meet the target price?

- Will customers respond negatively to the reduced performance or eliminated feature?
- Is the project on time for launch in July?
- Do we need to change our original target specs to meet the proposed introduction date?
- Can we get the margins back up to where we want them?
- Should we delay launch while we perfect the new technology?

These familiar issues came up on just about every project. Executives responsible for monitoring and approving projects considered these same questions over and over again. The same group of people at Axlerod addressed the same questions over and over again on each and every product development project—for years on end—yet made no fundamental changes in the nature of the decision process.

Oh, there were attempts. The first attempt was to meet more frequently so management could "keep a tighter rein" on each project. It was a sincere management effort to be of greater help to the teams. This additional attention barely changed the agenda at all. The product development activities simply consumed more and more of the executive group's time, and update meetings distracted the development teams and drew the executive group deeper and deeper into technical and tactical issues that they were less qualified to address than the project team.

The next attempt to improve the process at Axlerod was to recruit and hire a highly qualified executive to take over the product development activity. The person was located and hired, and for a while it seemed that things were improving. However, as projects got closer and closer to introduction, the executive group found that more and more of the vexing product changes and performance specifications had simply been changed within the product development group and were a "surprise" to other members of the executive group. The product they were presented with for approval at the eleventh hour was no longer the product they thought was being developed. The executive group could either send the product back to the development team, missing the introduction targets, or let it go forward in its modified and more questionable form—

frustrating choices, to say the least. The executive group was not satisfied with the hired expert approach. The product development executive was retained, but with vastly reduced autonomy.

The next attempt was to institute a process. A highly detailed process would keep things on track and prevent time-consuming and expensive problems. The "process" was documented, including every checkpoint and tollgate and the kinds and format of the information to be presented at each juncture. Lists and lists of questions were to be answered and verified by the project team. The development effort slowed to a crawl as each team studied the large binder outlining "the process" and meticulously completed each and every one of the forms, reports, communications, and questions. The process was awash in paper. The quality of the products being developed, however, improved not at all.

But the process certainly "looked" much more organized. It had become an exercise in filling out forms and completing reports for the tollgate meetings. Actual development sometimes seemed to be secondary to completing the specified paperwork. Specialists were devoted to "having everything ready" for the management presentations at each tollgate. What this process really accomplished was to spawn some highly creative writing skills. The kinds of issues really hadn't changed much (lower-than-desired performance, at higher-than-desired costs, delivered later than planned). But the justification, in considerable detail, for why the project was not going as planned was always presented. Despite these problems, the presenters always posed that everything was really just fine, or soon to be remedied. The rationalization was truly impressive. It would have made a career bureaucrat proud. But this approach was just another type of failure. In each situation the company tried to remedy what

> *If companies showed as much enthusiasm and creativity in designing products as they do in designing forms, they would be much better off.*

were thought to be obvious problems. They instituted "obvious" solutions. Each response seemed completely logical given the understanding of the problem at the time. And each response failed.

The solutions to persistent problems are seldom obvious. In the case of Axlerod Manufacturing, several critical considerations were apparently overlooked:

- When the target is unclear, "project criteria creep" (also sometimes called mission creep) is almost inevitable.
- The problems demanded considerably more precision from the executive group than they thought was required.
- The key criteria for product success should be set by the leadership of the company and not by the project team.
- Defining the administrative elements of the process does not necessarily improve the qualitative results of the process.
- Choice of team members depends on the level of challenge and strategic importance of the project. The team must be up to the challenge.
- A high-level charismatic leader is no guarantee of successful products.
- Working hard is not a substitute for working smart.

Many management groups find it extremely frustrating to have to deal with the same problems over and over again, on different projects and at different times. Often, however, this frustration can serve to make the executives feel involved. It may reinforce the feeling that they are "doing their job" by being in there making decisions that are familiar and are doing so in a

> *A small team of high-caliber creative talents will always outperform a larger group of less-talented individuals. But the high-caliber team operates best when given a tough challenge. Horses for courses.*

thoroughly executive manner. This is what executives are for—right? Wrong. The trouble at Axlerod and similar companies is just that they are using a poorly conceived and inefficient system to guide product development. It is slow, costly beyond belief, and thoroughly frustrating to the project team members. Everybody is trying to hit multiple moving targets, and it's never even quite clear why the targets are moving. Something better is needed. That something is the new product decision screen.

The New Product Decision Screen

The decision screen idea is founded on the premise that new product development is much better, cheaper, and faster when the executive group focuses on spending quality time developing specific and well-founded criteria for selecting new product development projects, rather than spending time trying to bring projects back on track when the project is almost completed. This requires the executive management group to understand precisely what drives product success at the company and then to provide this input to each product team in the form of a decision screen. Executive group members decide once precisely what criteria are acceptable, so they do not have to do so over and over. These criteria should remain constant so long as the current corporate strategy remains in effect.

A workable screen does not have to be long. In fact, it should seldom exceed two or three pages. The best screens cover several key decision areas:

- Target markets to be served
- Profit (margin) requirements
- Desired volume minimums
- Technologies to be optimized if appropriate
- Core competencies to exploit
- Favored competitive situations
- Weaknesses to avoid

These are not factors deserving only casual consideration. Each question requires considerable discussion and may require specific research to determine how it affects company performance. It is not an exercise in filling out forms. Each question calls for a concerted (and usually difficult) effort to truly understand what factors drive company performance.

Decision screens offer several persuasive advantages:

- Improved quality of key product decisions
- Fewer "obvious" problems for the executive group to decide (because the situations clearly do not meet the established criteria)
- Better understanding at the outset of staffing and funding requirements
- Vastly improved speed due to the absence of "restarts" and criteria changes
- Clear goals for each team

A word of caution is also in order. The decision screen is not just a wish list. The criteria must meet the strategic needs of the company, but they must also be reasonable and achievable. Setting goals too high to motivate product teams is invariably self-defeating. Impossible goals are not motivators; they merely guarantee failure, and the negative influences on the process and the individuals can be severe.

Should one find that the requirements for strategic success exceed the skill levels of existing personnel who must actually meet these requirements, then management must move to either develop, acquire, or contract out the necessary capabilities. Certainly it would be ridiculous to lower the strategic requirements to unacceptable levels just to coincide with the inadequate skills presently available for the development effort. The minimum criteria for market success do not vary with the resources available. It is essential that those responsible for directing corporate activity understand clearly what is actually required for market success.

Customer Targets

A recurring theme of this book is the necessity of clear customer targets. Here again, it is the number one criterion for the decision screen. If you go to all the trouble and expense to determine precisely whom your business is going to serve, under no circumstances should a project team work on satisfying customers outside the intended target. It is simply a waste of time, money, and talent. (This is a key element in team manufacturing strategy. Don't do things you will not get paid for.)

Choose your targets carefully. Stick to those targets. Insist that your employees stick to those targets. Reevaluate your targets every few years, but do not indulge in a running discussion of whom you should be serving.

Economic Criteria

Minimum profitability criteria should not be discussed and re-decided in every meeting. Simple as this sounds, it is not obvious, because some businesses seem to offer a sea of potential exceptions. Even so, the first question is which measure or measures will be your guide. Variable margin (direct materials and labor exclusive of overhead costs divided by net selling price) is one popular measure. Economic value added (EVA) is another. Some measure of return on invested capital (development costs necessary to bring a product to market) might be a chosen measure.

It is important that sufficient consideration be committed early so that when an expensive project comes in at the last minute with a projected 28 percent variable margin in lieu of the 30 percent minimum in the screen that the group can confidently and comfortably send the project back to the drawing board. The first time a project is approved at less than the established minimum, the word will travel like a bushfire that everything in the screen is really "negotiable," and each project team will begin creative work on a rationale for future negotiations.

> *We establish nonnegotiable conditions to ensure that people spend their time focusing on issues they can influence, rather than wasting time on less important issues. Well-designed constraints actually liberate!*

Minimum Efficient Sales Volume

In many situations there is a clear minimum profit/manufacturing volume, below which products or product lines simply tend to be more trouble than they are worth. Sometimes it's possible to define this minimum volume with great precision and with irrefutable evidence, but such precision isn't really necessary. Empirical data simply make the call a little easier.

One way to view the profit/volume issue is to develop a nine cell profit/volume matrix as shown in Figure 6-1. On the horizontal axis establish a minimum profit measure, anything below which the group would agree to be "low" profit. This is

> *The definition of "success" requires some minimum level of sales volume combined with an acceptable level of profitability.*

Figure 6-1. The profit/volume matrix.

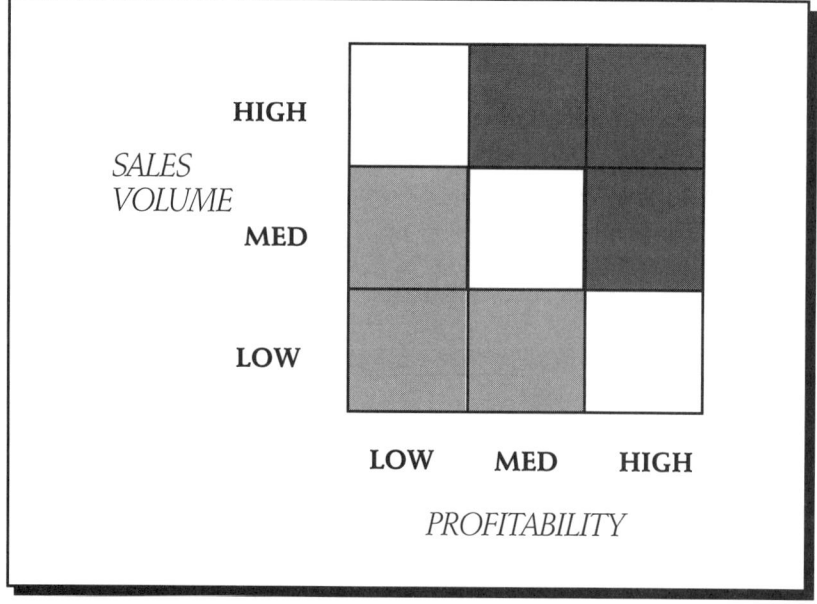

a category that the group should easily be able to determine to be unacceptable: "We don't want our products to fall in here." Next, establish a level anything above which the group would agree represents "high" profitability. This is not necessarily your target, but rather products falling herein clearly exceed expectations and are the best performers. By elimination, everything in between the low and the high represents "medium" profitability. The group now has three classes of product by profitability.

On the vertical axis go through the same process, first establishing that sales volume anything below which the group agrees is undesirably low. Repeat the same process to determine the level that would be considered a "high volume product," possibly the top 20 percent of products. The team can now plot existing products or lines on the matrix. The process is usually quite illuminating.

The point is to gain understanding of your basic product economics in a way that sheds light on the proper minimum criteria for success and at the same time secures a view of past product performance. The managers of one company found the sudden awareness compelling so they essentially decided they needed to replace nearly all of their existing products if they were to become the company described in their goal statements.

Core Competencies to Emphasize

Every organization has some things it does better than others. It may or may not do these things well enough to actually survive, but these are the things the organization does best. Ideally, an organization also possesses one or more "distinctive competencies," something it does better than any of its competitors.

Certainly these are the things you should try to take advantage of, as opposed to trying to make products that require all new skills and at which you are totally untested. Such an approach merely serves to improve the probability of success. You do not want to take risks that are not necessary to achieve your goals. There are always risks. You simply want to avoid the unnecessary ones.

The objective here is to be as specific as possible. You should look for "generic" skills that you can capitalize on—something like, "We are able to rollform steel sheet more efficiently than any competitor in our industry." It doesn't mean that every desirable new product will use that technology, but you always want to keep in mind what you do well.

Weaknesses to Avoid

It is desirable to go through a very thorough exercise to develop an understanding of corporate weaknesses. Usually, not everyone in the group will agree on every item. It's important, however, that the group reach a clear understanding and some level of consensus on what constitutes a strategic weakness.

Every company, for reasons of its historical experience, or just its evolved cultural inclinations, will have things it simply does not do well. The reasons for the weaknesses are unimportant for this exercise. The purpose is to agree on things you should avoid.

Favorable Competitive Conditions to Exploit

Just what constitutes favorable competitive conditions is probably a worthwhile discussion for any management group, but it is doubly important to understand those conditions under which your organization usually prevails—and those where it doesn't.

Appendix I provides a sample format and example of a decision screen.

It should be obvious that before you can develop a useful decision screen, you must already have worked out such fundamen-

> *A word of caution. Slavish devotion to a simple core competence is dangerous. It is like owning only a hammer, and hence seeing every problem as a nail.*

tal details as clear mission statement, goals, and strategic direction.

Along the same line, if your organization has attempted to establish decision criteria in the past and had little success, it is likely that the fundamental strategic questions are inadequately clear or have been abandoned. Now is the time to clarify those strategic questions.

Summary

A well-crafted new product decision screen can save management a great deal of time while simultaneously improving the general level of new product decision making. Rehashing the same questions each time a new product opportunity arises is always inefficient, and frequently results in inconsistent responses to similar situations.

By taking the time to set the performance criteria necessary for a successful product, management can take an important step toward providing innovative new products that are not only successful, but can be brought to market faster. Why build a new wrench for each successive 1/2" bolt we need to tighten?

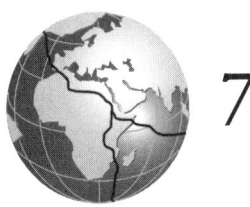

7

Staffing the Development Activity

Current management literature often suggests that the self-directed project team is the preferred form of organization for doing virtually anything. Successful products can be created under just about any rational form of organization, however. That certainly includes teams, self-directed or otherwise. It's much more important that the method fit the organizational personality of the company than the mantra of any book or article on organization. Should one choose the team approach, however—and it is indeed a good choice for many situations—it is equally important that the individual members of the project team be carefully chosen.

Teams Aren't the Only Choice

Basically, there are several common forms of organization for product development activities:

- Functional organization
- Matrix organization
- Dedicated project team
- Ad hoc project teams
- Self-directed project team

Each of these organizational units can be successful, and each has its own strengths and weaknesses. Smaller organizations, of course, may be much more limited in their choices than large corporations. Many small companies cannot assemble even a single multidisciplinary team. They simply do not have such dedicated specialists within the company, let alone enough of them to devote to dedicated product development projects.

Such companies often buy their new products from inventors or designers and proceed from there. Others copy the products of their competitors. Often, the smaller manufacturer's product portfolio is a jumble of products obtained from various sources. Our concern here is with the organization that is capable of fielding at least a rudimentary project development effort internally. For such a company, any one of the following organizational forms may be appropriate.

Functional Organization

The functional method of organization is nothing more than the traditional approach with which most readers are familiar. The marketing department does the marketing chores under the direction of the head of that department. Engineering is undertaken by the engineering department under the head of that function. Industrial design is conducted under its own department head. Manufacturing personnel usually find out what they are supposed to make well after the design is conceived or even completed. Coordination is done principally by the managers, who then pass the chores on to their staffs.

Matrix Organization

The matrix organization entails a higher level of coordination among the various disciplines. Typically, personnel are drawn from each of the functional departments on an as-needed basis and may fall temporarily under the jurisdiction of the project leader while their services are needed. Usually, the formal reporting relationship remains with the functional department head, even though the individual is actually working for the project leader.

Staffing the Development Activity

The matrix organization is generally believed to be more flexible than the functional organization, but recent experience has shown that the desired flexibility is usually not as forthcoming as one would hope. Because responsibility and loyalty still lie with the functional department—and not the specific project—political squabbles often erupt, which leave the individual employees with conflicting loyalties. Matrix approaches can work, but in many organizations they are not the ideal form.

Dedicated Project Team

In recent years the dedicated project team has become much more common. In this situation a core team reports to someone responsible for completing the project. This person could be a marketing executive, an engineering or manufacturing executive, or an executive dedicated to new product development.

Individual team members relinquish reporting relationships to their former functional department heads and become full-time members of the project team for the duration of the project—often an extended period. When the project is completed, the team members are free to return to their old job, to a different job in the functional department, or to another project group. Project-team work assignments are frequently seen as paths to promotion in many organizations, because it is an opportunity for the team members to distinguish themselves through new and challenging assignments.

Self-Directed Project Team

The self-directed project team is a variation on the dedicated project team. However, in the case of the self-directed team, as the name implies, the team has a much higher level of autonomy within the hierarchical organization. In essence, the team manages and governs itself. Such groups can work extremely well in cases where the members and the challenges are well suited to each other.

The self-directed team can perform well if there is a clear sense of direction and defined performance criteria (such as that discussed in Chapter 6 on decision screens). Lack of clear direction, purpose, and performance criteria can make a real muddle out of an otherwise capable self-directed team. Clear direction and an occasional sense of urgency are needed to unite and motivate a self-directed team.

Ad Hoc Project Teams

Another useful variant of the project team, ad hoc teams are less formal and usually less permanent than dedicated and self-directed teams. Ad hoc teams are most successful when solving specific technical or operational challenges. Often the team members are a subset of the larger project team and have been grouped to address specific issues. When the specific challenges are met, the team is disbanded.

Staffing Requirements

General staffing guidelines can save you a lot of grief—and money. There are several essential requirements for staffing a successful product development effort:

- Multidisciplinary skills
- Personality compatibility among group members
- Understanding of how the project relates to the strategic plan
- Effective project leadership
- The smallest possible development team

When these requirements are satisfied, the group has a strong opportunity to achieve success. If only one of the requirements is missing, the probability of trouble increases dramatically. When two are missing, the results are almost guaranteed to be mediocre at best.

In his memoirs, Field Marshall B. L. Montgomery outlined a staffing philosophy that he attributed to a member of the German General Staff.[1] It divided people into four distinct types:

1. *The Brilliant and Active.* These folks made the finest field commanders. They are very rare, and when one finds them, they should be used carefully.
2. *The Brilliant and Lazy.* This group was thought to produce the best staff officers. Because they were lazy, they were always looking for the easiest way to do everything. Because they were very smart, the ideas were usually good ones. Just what is needed for superior staff work.
3. *The Stupid and Lazy.* Not really much to be concerned with. Yes, they're not very bright, but they don't really do anything either, so they don't cause much mischief. They can usually be ignored with little ill effect (except for their cost, of course, which is of more concern to a commercial company than to an army).
4. *The Stupid and Active.* Get rid of them immediately. They don't know how to do anything—but they are tireless and always busy doing it! They cause continual and often irreparable damage if not dealt with promptly.

Although one may not subscribe to this taxonomy of human nature, it is at least a provocative take on staff selection and retention.

Selecting the development group is one of the key decisions management will make. Yet the actual selection of group members is frequently delegated, with the assumption that the right resources are, in fact, available in the company and that they will be assigned to the project. In reality, nothing could be further from the truth in many organizations.

Well-intentioned senior management may go to great lengths to develop a strategic plan, and that plan may be quite specific about the role of new products in the corporate strategies. They may make ample provision for funding the development projects. In short, they may get off to a good start—only then to make erroneous assumptions about the human element and the skills required.

Some of these mistaken assumptions may result from the natural desire to show confidence in the company's employees. In fact, in almost every strategic planning activity the authors have facilitated, there has been a notable tendency to claim that the company has "the best employees in the business." Such loyalty, either real or imagined, is commendable, but it does nothing to help form an objective appraisal of the requirements for successfully creating the new products called for in the strategic plan. It is an essential element of executive responsibility to ensure that the company has the human resources necessary to execute the strategies they create.

Because the teams that effect the best, most productive, and most successful development efforts are typically multidisciplinary, no single functional executive is usually intimately familiar with all of the proposed group members. It is not unreasonable to treat the assignment of human resources with as much care as the allocation of financial resources. It should stand to reason that one cannot create world-class products with second-class skills.

Multidisciplinary Skills

No matter how you organize, you need multidisciplinary inputs to the new product development process. These inputs are normally functional skills:

- *Technical.* Design and engineering.
- *Marketing.* Customer, pricing, promotional, and distribution elements.
- *Procurement.* Suppliers of both materials and technology.
- *Manufacturing/Operations.* Process elements.

- *Technical Inputs.* Most manufactured products require engineering input of one type or another. If those appointed to fulfill this role are not technically qualified for the challenge at hand, then the project is almost certainly destined to failure. In organizations that develop products on an irregular basis, development engineers are often chosen from operating departments to fill these temporary development roles. It is not uncommon for line management to hold back the best people (the ones for whom they are personally responsible and on whose performance they are personally evaluated) for ongoing operations. For the overall benefit of the organization, however, the most capable, most innovative, and most productive people should be appointed to generate the profits of the future. They must also be *technically qualified* to create the product using the most appropriate materials and methods.

○ *Marketing Inputs.* In recent years it has become more common to include marketing input in the earliest stages of product development and to have a marketing representative as a permanent full-time team member. For many decades previously, and probably well into the eighties, it was uncommon to find a marketing professional working in product development shoulder to shoulder with an engineer. The marketing professional can bring a great deal to the party, however.

Almost invariably, a product's success is enhanced by early involvement of a skilled marketing professional. If you wait until the product is ready to market, it's too late to affect pricing strategy or distribution concerns or to take advantage of unique advantages integral to the product for creative pricing, distribution, or promotion.

Often there are product features that, although not strictly necessary, add greatly to the promotion or "story" used to promote and sell the product. Such promotion enhancers may be added at little or no cost when conceived early on but may require complete redesign to add later. The impact on market introduction can be substantial.

○ *Procurement Resource.* For products requiring numerous material inputs, it is advantageous to have ongoing procurement involvement. Alternative materials may offer substantial cost advantages, and often the procurement specialist who is in frequent contact with vendors trying to promote alternative materials can save the day. In cases where it's not possible or feasible to have a full-time procurement specialist on the project, close lines of communication with the appropriate procurement experts may suffice.

Many projects and designs become too far advanced before someone realizes that manufacturing is working with a less than ideal material or source. It should be the responsibility of the procurement specialist to see that this does not happen.

○ *Manufacturing/Operations.* Companies that create their products in the absence of direct manufacturing involvement are missing a huge opportunity. The people who will ultimately have to make the products should have input into development. There is simply no substitute for input from the shop floor. Even the best engineers and designers, who may know a great deal about the manufacturing technology and processes, are unlikely to be intimately familiar with the day-to-day mundane problems that those who actually make the stuff have to deal with.

Some years ago a large manufacturing company introduced a new and spectacularly successful office chair. It was extremely well designed and available in many colors and materials. Because the product was going into highly design-sensitive applications, it was specified by the design department with five shades of black plastic shell colors. There was a warm black, a cool black, and so on. It sounded like a great idea to the industrial design department and also to specifiers in the marketplace.

When the products were being produced, however, it became all but impossible for those selecting the parts on the line to tell the difference between the various shades of black. Each chair contained several black plastic parts that had to match. Even in a well-lighted and state-of-the-art factory environment, color selection errors were made regularly. Chairs were continually going out with mismatched shell parts, and field repair was extremely costly, not to mention the damage to the company's reputation for quality.

After about a year of fighting this problem, manufacturing finally prevailed and persuaded the marketing department to reduce the five colors of black to a single black color. There was no adverse market reaction, and a major manufacturing hassle was eliminated. Had there been knowledgeable plant input early on, the problem would have been identified in plenty of time to be avoided prior to market introduction.

Small Development Team

When the number of people directly involved in a product development project—or in any project—gets larger than absolutely necessary, the problems of communication, misunderstanding, conflict, and competing ideas increase exponentially.

Of course, it is possible to manage projects involving large

Staffing the Development Activity

numbers of people. To do so, however, usually requires management procedures that are much more demanding. Why make the problem harder than it already is?

Compatible Personalities

It is not always possible to have available the perfect personnel choices for every project. Some very creative people can be somewhat difficult or eccentric. Although eliminating the best talent to achieve harmony is usually not feasible, whoever selects the team members should keep in mind that developing a new product frequently becomes a very intense business as team members resolve competing ideas and concepts as they progress toward the goal. The more compatible the personalities are, the easier these difficult situations will be and the less chance there will be of a major project collapse. See Figures 7-1 and 7-2.

The Importance of "Process"

Normal tensions affiliated with product development can be reduced dramatically by the presence of a structured process that emphasizes facts and information over emotion and opinion.

As discussed in Chapter 1 and elsewhere, a structured process is one of the three critical elements of new product development. Even the best team benefits from knowledge of a repeatable process. This is not to advocate some mindless repetition of steps defined by someone who is not actively participating in the development effort at hand. To the contrary, the process is clearly a guide, an aid to already competent team members that makes their job easier.

If the team finds that the process is too oppressive, there is probably something wrong with the process. It is not unusual

> *It should not be surprising if a design team large enough to design an armored vehicle designs a toaster that looks and performs like a tank.*

Figure 7-1. Incompatible personalities on a team.

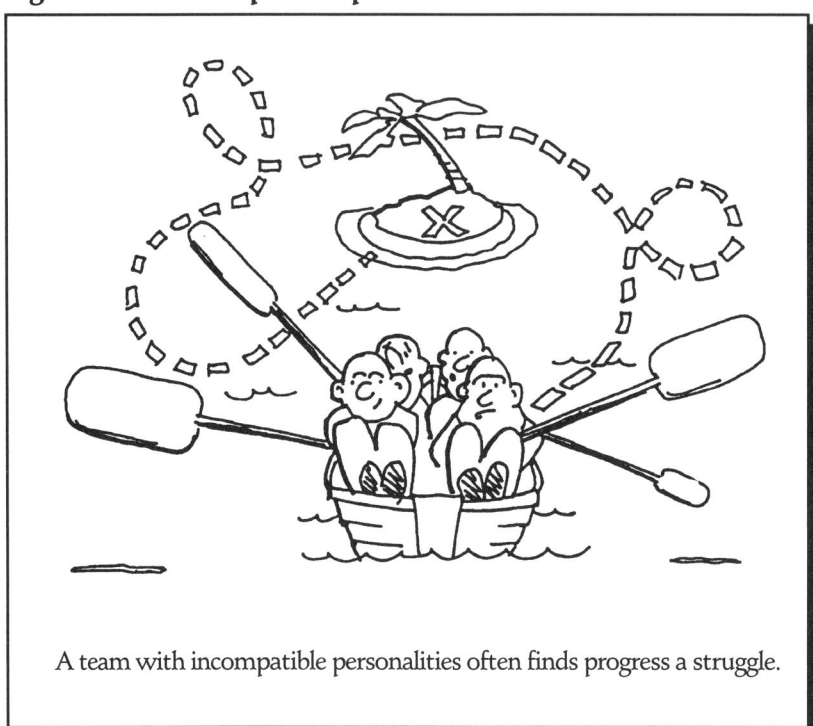

A team with incompatible personalities often finds progress a struggle.

for team members to exhibit some resistance to any procedures that reduce their perceived freedom of action. Coincidentally, a really good development process does not limit action or freedom so much as it assists the members in repeating success.

Involving Customers and Other Contributors

It would be premature to leave the topic of setting up the product development process without addressing the valuable contribution that customers and others outside the company can make. You should include persons directly involved in the specification, use, installation, distribution, or repair of your products whenever possible. Companies with long-standing repeat cus-

Figure 7-2. Compatible personalities on a team.

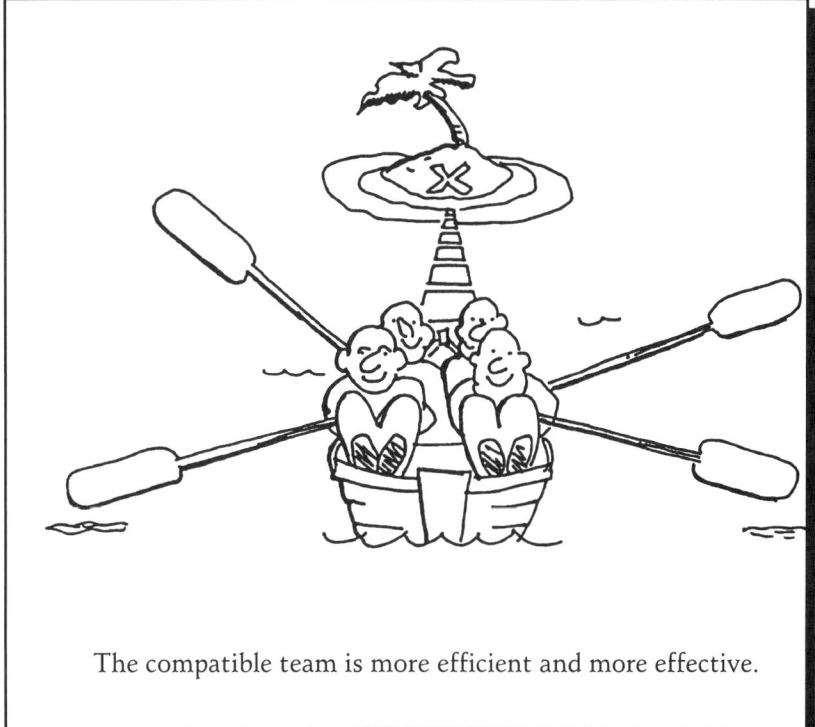

The compatible team is more efficient and more effective.

tomers may find such collaboration relatively easy. Companies with customers who purchase huge quantities of their product will find more customers willing to invest time in their development efforts.

Outside contributors are unlikely to be full-time team members, but if development team members try to make it as easy as possible for customers and others to contribute, they will find them much more responsive to their invitations for involvement. Some customers find it "fun" to help if it doesn't take up too much time or money. Some find it in their interest to invest in input to get their specific problems or needs addressed.

Such involvement may well guarantee a customer when the product is available. It is difficult to envision a situation in which closeness to the customer would be more productive.

Summary

The choice of organization for new product development is an individual one. The trend to multidisciplinary teams is a good one when sufficient resources can be mustered to the project. When the complete complement of resources is not available for every project, then other approaches might be necessary. There is little doubt, however, that most projects benefit from the input of the diverse disciplines of marketing, engineering, design, procurement, manufacturing, and finance.

The choice of team members is important. Competence is essential, but compatibility, or the lack thereof, can mean the difference between a smoothly functioning team and dismal failure. The authors place particular importance on the active involvement of engineering and manufacturing in the design team, not because these folks are more creative or innovative than others, but because ultimately the product must be produced. Otherwise, great products that cannot be manufactured efficiently are almost always failures. Smaller teams are generally preferable to larger teams whenever possible, simply because the smaller the team, the more efficient and effective the internal communication.

Note

1. Bernard Law, Viscount Montgomery of Alemain, *The Memoirs of Field-Marshall the Viscount Montgomery of Alemain K.G.* (London: Collins St. James Place, 1958).

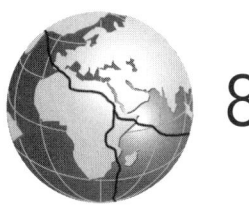

8

Managing Existing Products and Markets

Because few companies find their product portfolio and customer base "ideal" when they implement a strategic approach to new product development, changes and improvements are always a topic of discussion. What happens to existing products and customers when new ones come into the picture? How does one apply the principles outlined so far to restructuring existing products and markets?

Managing What You Already Have

A proper evaluation of existing products and markets involves several considerations. The primary issues are the following:

- Do existing customers and products fit with the current corporate strategy?
- How does the current customer base compare with the "target" customer segments?
- What happens to those customers who do not fit our target segments?
- Is the current product mix appropriate to the target segments' needs?
- Are there opportunities for a "platform" strategy?

- How does the company make the transition to the desired product mix?

Corporate Strategy and Customer/Product Analysis

A carefully crafted corporate strategy should determine those activities that must follow. Oddly, it seems that many managers draw an arbitrary line between current products and customers and the strategic plan intended to drive the future. All attention is directed to future activities, and existing customer misfits and current product deficiencies are passed over.

The goal, however, should be to reach the desired mix of target customers with profitable, high-value products that can be efficiently and easily manufactured. The strategic plan should take both the current customer and product mix and the future strategic direction into account in the process of continual improvement. It is essentially a matter of making progress in the desired direction while simultaneously taking advantage of those opportunities, sometimes enormous, that present themselves in the form of current products and current customers. It is entirely possible for a company to find that it can make greater economic and strategic returns by correcting existing deficiencies than by launching completely new solutions. To determine

> *Whatever future plans a company may have, the fact is that it has current customers and products to deal with.*

> *It is often possible to realize larger returns by addressing existing deficiencies than by launching completely new solutions.*

the best approach in each case, one needs to do a little investigative work. The first step is to examine the existing customer base.

Analyzing Existing Customer Segments

If you have not already performed an analysis of existing customer and market segments as part of the strategic planning effort, now is the right time. By this stage, you should have available both a workable market segmentation model and a relatively clear view of the customer segments that offer the most attractive opportunities. In other words, you know pretty clearly whom the company wants to do business with.

The next logical step is to examine current customers in light of the segmentation model. How close is the current customer base to that desired? This generally involves two primary steps:

1. Identifying all existing customers and fitting them into the market segments defined in the model
2. Determining how to handle those that are outside the target segments

The first step should be rather straightforward if your company has customer (end user) sales records, although it may be tedious if the customer base is large. If the number is clearly unmanageable via a census type approach, sampling of sales records may be employed. Be sure to use sound methods of sampling to ensure that your sample is unbiased and thus accurate enough to allow you to make some important decisions. The key question is, "Are the vast majority of our customers in the segments we wish to target?" A worksheet for recording the results of this analysis is provided in Figure 8-1.

Every company probably gets *some* business from custom-

The first step is to determine precisely whom you are doing business with now.

Figure 8-1. Customer/segment analysis.

Customer Name	Segment	Target		Disposition	Comments
		YES	NO		
1.					
2.					
3.					
4.					
5.					
6.					
7.					

Managing Existing Products and Markets

ers outside its primary target segments. This is nothing to worry about if the percentage is, say, 10 percent or less. If more than 10 percent of your sales are coming from customers outside your target segments, something is out of kilter, and the company will undoubtedly benefit from adjustments. The point is that no company is likely to receive 100 percent of its business from its primary target segments only.

Not every company is lucky enough to have in-house sales records that identify end users and relate these to its segment model. In these cases it is necessary to obtain the information the best way one can. For example, it may be possible to obtain user information from retailers' records (although you may have to foot the bill for extracting the information). Warranty cards are one of the most popular means of getting the information and are used only occasionally for warranty decisions. In effect, you have to go where the information is; if it's necessary to conduct surveys or in-store sampling, then that may be the only way to learn what you need to know. But you do need to know with at least a moderate degree of accuracy.

The customer decision (whether to retain a customer outside your target segments or sacrifice the sales volume) will be linked to the product decisions discussed later on in this chapter. They are interdependent in the sense that deletion of a product or line for reasons of process or manufacturing efficiency may be the determining factor in how to handle purchasers of that product. If the customer is within the target segments emphasized, there is a very good chance that you can convert the customer to another product (either new or existing).

Customers falling outside company target segments and for which there is no logical and good product or service solution may have to be referred to another source of product in the most helpful and amicable manner possible. The very essence of strategic target-

> *Ideally, you want to keep the existing customers, but with a better, more profitable product.*

ing is the premise that you do not try to do business with everyone. It may not be desirable to maintain every customer.

Analyzing Current Products

After examining your current customer base for agreement with your target customer segments, you need to determine which current products are a good fit for your corporate strategy. You need to answer three questions:

1. Which products can be retained without alteration?
2. Which products could (and should) be altered or improved to fit current target segments?
3. Which products should be deleted?

Which products can be retained without alteration? In the best scenario, most existing products fall into this category and can be retained without alteration. It is important, however, to provide an objective analysis on which to base your decisions. The process is relatively straightforward but does involve some number crunching.

Products that can be retained without alteration are those that meet the same criteria used for the new product decision screen, discussed in Chapter 6. Essentially, they meet the volume, profit, process, and customer target criteria.

It is particularly important to determine precisely who is currently purchasing each product or line to ensure that you do not decide to retain a product that is purchased only by non-target customers.

Which products could and should be altered or improved to fit current target segments? Products that meet the needs of a target

> *An objective decision support tool like the new product decision screen makes the decision process easier.*

segment but are lacking in one or more *minor* respects are candidates for modification. The military axiom to "never reinforce failure" is applicable here. Bad products are bad products, and you should not reengineer a genuine loser, no matter how much the company may have invested in it or how much a member of management may like the product.

In some cases, establishing or improving a product "platform" creates the opportunity to correct product defects and simultaneously reduce parts and assemblies, thus improving the manufacturability of the products.

Which products should be deleted? Many products hang on way too long before they are replaced in the product lineup. If the existing product does not serve a target segment or no longer meets the current new product decision screen, it should be deleted.

There is no virtue in throwing good money after bad. The new product decision screen should be the ultimate arbiter of questionable products. A good decision screen makes it clear whether a product fits the criteria or not. It should be unambiguous. Let the losers go and move on to something more productive. Focus on getting it right the next time.

The authors have seen one situation where it was necessary to replace virtually all of the company's products to reach the desired customer/product mix. The profitable, big-selling product lines were all declining rapidly. The more recently developed replacements were all sadly defective in manufacturability and customer acceptance. Profitability on the most recent products was miserable.

Unfortunately, this company was confronted with the situation where reengineering and redesigning the deficient products would have involved nearly as much time and money as replacing them with brand-new, properly developed products. This realization was, of course, more than a little painful for management.

After much analysis and consideration, the company committed to completely replacing its product offerings over a three- to five-year period. This was a bold and ultimately successful undertaking.

Analyzing Product Segments

Different types of products do, of course, demand somewhat different handling in terms of analysis, but it's possible to offer some guidance without attempting to exhaust all the possibilities.

Figure 8-2 shows a sample worksheet for conducting a product line analysis. It might be desirable to attach values to each factor, with a simple spreadsheet program rapidly doing the calculations to provide a common rating scale of desirability.

Under no circumstances should the analysis and rating criteria be in direct conflict with the criteria for the new product decision screen. Each should directly support the corporate strategy with respect to target markets served and product acceptability criteria.

When appropriate, analysis of product lines (as opposed to individual models) can save considerable work. If the entire line is a misfit, it makes little sense to go into great analytical detail examining individual models.

The worksheet shown in Figure 8-2 is just a simple way of displaying the key information needed to decide the product line's future. Following are some considerations:

- What percentage of sales are made to targeted segments?
- What is the sales volume of the line? Is it a big seller or just an also-ran? It might also be useful to include a column showing the stage of the product life cycle for the line (i.e., introduction, growth, maturity, or decline).
- Is this a profitable line, or is it below the new product screen criteria?
- Is this a growing or a declining line?
- How efficient is this line to manufacture? Do production processes run smoothly, or is this line always a problem?
- Tentatively, what is the recommended disposition: retain as is, retain with modifications, or delete immediately, or when feasible?

If a product line legitimately qualifies for redesign or upgrading, then it's appropriate to move on to the next level of

Figure 8-2. Product line analysis.

Product line	% Target	$ Volume	Profitability	Growth Rate	Complexity Factor	Disposition	Comments
1.							
2.							
3.							
4.							
5.							
6.							
7.							

analysis to determine just what types of changes would be beneficial. This analysis is only a beginning. It will help to determine the business issues, but it will not offer specific design solutions. Figure 8-3 shows a sample worksheet for this next level of analysis.

You will probably have some ideas about what needs to be changed before you conduct the detailed line analysis. It is always a mistake, however, to leap at the seemingly obvious solutions without carefully examining the facts. If you are going to make changes or improvements in the line, this is the ideal opportunity to get everything right and avoid another redo later. This is the time to fix it.

The best way to proceed with major line changes is to approach the project just like a new product, appointing a multidisciplinary team. The only real difference is that you have the benefit of some experience with the line. It should be much easier to optimize manufacturing concerns in this type of project. Although the primary concern, of course, is to match the line with your target segment customers, it would be false economy to miss this opportunity to increase manufacturability, profitability, and acceptability all at the same time.

Ongoing Management and Reporting Systems

If you do not have an effective product management system in place, now is a good time to implement one. You have just gone through most of the work in establishing the criteria for product performance and manufacturability, so why not take advantage of the work already done and extend it into a formal product management information system? Although such a system is beyond the scope of this book, every company should have a system to provide necessary and accurate decision information.

Opportunities for a "Platform" Strategy

The topic of product "platforms" has received considerable discussion over the past few years. The term simply implies that it is beneficial to establish a fundamental structural architecture

Figure 8-3. Detailed product line analysis.

Model	Unit Volume	$ Volume	Profitability	Growth Rate	Complexity Factor	Disposition	Comments
1.							
2.							
3.							
4.							
5.							
6.							
7.							

> *A major product line redesign may involve more resources than some new products.*

> *A platform strategy can be extremely powerful.*

(the product platform) from which various lines are efficiently spawned through relatively simple (to produce) changes in visuals, options, features, or performance levels.

Benefits include increased simplicity of manufacture, fewer parts and subassemblies, lower inventory levels, and reduced training times. Platform strategies can produce sizable gains in profitability and reduced manufacturing costs when they are employed in a manner acceptable to the customer segments targeted.

Making the Transition to the Desired Product Mix

In evaluating today's products in the context of tomorrow's target customers, you should keep in mind that you are restructuring some of today's resources to fit tomorrow's needs. You want to create a smooth and efficient transition from where the company is currently to where you want it to be.

To do so requires looking to the future while working assiduously in the present—always working *toward* the goal.

Let's assume that the hypothetical Newco Manufacturing

> *A carefully structured transition plan is crucial if you want to prevent pandemonium during a major restructuring effort.*

Company has completed all of the foregoing steps and, as one might commonly expect to find in an average company, only about 40 percent of its current product lines are really good fits with its newly determined target market segments. Not surprisingly, these are pretty much the most successful and profitable products, which are sold mostly to the customers they were aimed at.

Another 35 percent of existing product lines are "disciplinary problems." Management may like these lines, but they don't sell as well as expected and probably have some profitability problems as well. Some customers really seem to like them. Sales reports, however, that many customers cannot be interested in these products even with price concessions and special service offers. Despite all this, the lines are worth keeping, but they need minor or major refinement to really be successful.

The remaining 25 percent simply do not make the cut. Some of these might have been pet projects of a particular executive "champion" but didn't sell as forecast. Others might have been rushed projects that weren't well thought out at all. Still others might have been special or custom products that were requested by a major customer and that management thought would make a cheap standard product for the mass market (a particularly attractive scenario because the first customer would essentially pay all the development costs). Whatever the reason, these products do not fit the criteria necessary to succeed in Newco's chosen target segments. Revising or reengineering these lines would be either too costly or ineffective. They will have to be dropped.

Newco is also typical in that it simply cannot make all the necessary product changes and replacements at one time. So how should the company proceed? How can it restructure its product portfolio without suffering a big reduction in sales volume from the deletion of the misfit lines? Every situation is somewhat different, of course, but there are some principles that can be applied to most situations to considerable benefit.

First, Newco should not just dump a big part of its sales volume without first arranging for the means to replace that volume. Two of the principal methods for achieving this are (1) to create a structured program to convert customers of the undesirable lines to other solutions in Newco's portfolio and (2) to develop new product lines or solutions to retain those targeted desirable customers that cannot be converted to other existing lines.

Next, Newco could develop a "transition strategy" that would provide it with a road map for the following:

- Repacing the sales volume lost through product line consolidation
- Determining in what order new and revised products must come on line prior to deletion of existing products
- Retaining existing desirable business through focused selling efforts to convert customers to other existing products or new products that will be coming down the pipeline

If a platform strategy makes sense for Newco, now would be the time to develop it. Newco would need to decide:

- How many "platforms" are appropriate to reconcile effective marketing with efficient manufacturing
- Whether all new products will fit the platforms
- What degree of commonality will exist across all platforms

Newco should also develop a product plan to guide the various development and redesign activities. Such a product plan should, at minimum, outline:

- The number and scope of projected product projects
- The desired product portfolio Newco is seeking to achieve

Summary

A major restructuring challenge does not have to mean mass confusion or sales loss as a result of replacing current products with new ones. The approach to existing product market analysis is to methodically see that your products are in fact serving the target segments you wish to serve, then making any minor adjustments that might be desirable. The whole purpose is to become properly aligned with the needs of your chosen customers. Those products that do not serve target customers must be replaced with ones that will, because keeping misaligned products merely distracts the company from its chosen targets. It may take some time to methodically implement the changes, possibly several years.

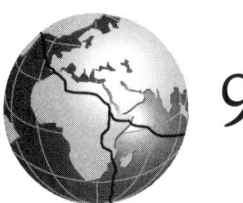

9

Analyzing New Product Opportunities

In the executive offices of companies throughout the world, literally thousands of capable and highly compensated executives gather to consider the "opportunities" brought before them. Some of these proposals are truly exemplary. Many, however, represent barely adequate to mediocre uses for corporate capital and would do little more than disperse important resources in ways that would virtually ensure little or no strategic impact. Most of the opportunities presented probably should not be undertaken at all.

Finding the Best—Not Just the Next—Opportunity

Some of these companies have highly developed processes for selecting the opportunities they pursue. Most have a selection "procedure" that appears to be rigorously structured and but falls far short of ensuring consistent success. There are several common shortcomings in selecting opportunities that every company should seek to avoid:

- Simply waiting for "opportunities" to appear
- Selecting only from the universe of opportunities that do simply "appear"

- Encouraging purveyors of opportunity proposals to set the criteria for success

Such a passive approach to opportunities invariably results in selecting too many small projects of little strategic value, creating a good deal of "feel good" activity but ultimately contributing little to profitability. Companies imbued with a sense of the strategic have little trouble focusing on opportunities that will continually and inexorably better their market position and corporate value.

Achieving Strategic Focus

Many companies operate without the benefit of a formal strategic plan. Many more go through the motions of planning but pay little attention to what was agreed upon as the relentless day-to-day activities steadily regain superiority over the strategic. Failure to manage according to the strategic plan is not only an acknowledgment of the ineffectiveness of the planning process but also a waste of one of the most powerful vehicles for focusing corporate operations. Everything, and especially opportunity selection, should completely and directly support the goals and strategies established in the strategic plan.

When the strategic plan ceases to be the source and focus of activity, priorities become less clear, middle managers become unsure of the exact direction, and the probability of missteps multiplies. A good plan, always kept in mind and continually reinforced, provides a guide and focus that simply cannot be achieved in any other manner.

Generating Opportunities

Numerous writers have maintained that there are enough "ideas" within most companies to generate all of the new product proposals that can be considered. It is doubtful, however, that the best opportunities will surface if management just solicits inputs. Such an approach may indeed generate an avalanche of inputs, but if the contributors lack the knowledge of precisely where the company is going and how it intends to get there, the proposals will probably not be the best opportunities, certainly not from a strategic perspective.

Soliciting input from everyone and then using none of it may also cause employees to question management's sincerity when their ideas are not pursued. Using an active approach to focus the attention of contributors and launching specific initiatives to discover optimal opportunities usually produces superior results.

Opportunity Analysis

The best opportunities are determined by the careful and rigorous work done in crafting corporate strategy. Opportunity analysis is merely a means of ensuring that the proposal selected best supports achievement of the goals specified in the strategic plan.

For this analysis to be successful, it is essential that the strategic plan be well crafted. The moment an opportunity appears that is obviously superior to the strategies outlined in the plan, the plan comes into question. A skillfully crafted strategic program should seldom encounter such "opportunity" surprises. Following is a look at how the major elements of a strategic plan guide opportunity analysis.

○ *The Mission Statement.* The mission statement should be much more than a promotion device to show potential and exist-

> *The objective should be to seek the best strategic opportunities, not just settle for the next opportunity.*

> *"A man must make his own opportunity, as oft as find it."—Francis Bacon*

ing customers how "hip" the company is. It should be more than a vehicle for motivating employees through banners and slogans. The mission statement should literally define the reason for the company's existence.

If the mission statement is not carefully and accurately drafted, it will either be ignored or, worse, become a source of confusion within the organization. Warm, fuzzy statements that no one believes are not helpful. There should be no contradiction, real or apparent, between the mission and the actions of the company. A company that does not truly believe its own mission statement is unlikely to demonstrate much more clarity in the planning efforts that flow from this starting point.

○ *Strategic Goals.* The best strategic goals are (1) few, (2) clear, (3) quantitative, and (4) measurable. Goals that say little more than "Go forth and do good works" are worse than useless. Too often there is a tendency to think that by slightly blurring the goal some future embarrassment might be avoided should the best efforts fall a bit short. But even the slightest fogging of the goals precipitates hedging throughout the remainder of the organization. When everyone can claim misses as successes, there is no accountability at all. Clear goals emanate from the top.

Following are four key measures that can serve as strategic goals:

- ○ A profitability target
- ○ A size or share target
- ○ A return on equity goal (such as EVA)
- ○ A shareholder value goal

The precise measure may vary somewhat according to the type of business, but some measure of each of these four key criteria is highly desirable. Each should be stated as a "hard target," not a range or an approximation. It is essential to know precisely how progress is unfolding and to know when the goals are achieved. If the measures aren't clear, how can one know when they have been achieved?

○ *Corporate Strategies.* Corporate strategies determine the basic direction of corporate activity. These are large and grand strategies. They are not, as Churchill stated, "small schemes." Corporate strategies are also relatively few in number (operational details have no place here) and clearly and simply stated. It should be absolutely clear to anyone likely to read the plan precisely what is intended. If a strategy takes more than 20 or 25 words to state clearly, then it's not clearly conceived.

Here are some examples of clear strategy statements:

- To increase our share in segment A to 25 percent through an emphasis on innovative, high-value products and personal service
- To reduce operating costs to 70 percent of sales by FY 20xx
- To replace existing residential product offerings with new, high-value offerings based on common product platforms by FY 20xx
- To increase sales in segment B by $800 million by FY 20xx through the conversion of competitors' customers to our products

It should be easy for those charged with implementing the many activities (usually outlined in the "operating plans") to know when they are, in fact, directly serving one of the corporate strategies. Opportunity analysis is one means of directly linking corporate strategies to the choice of opportunities.

Determining the Nature of the Opportunity

Any rigorous opportunity analysis requires a clear understanding of precisely what is being proposed. The initial scope of the opportunity should include reasonably accurate information with respect to the following:

- A clear definition of the opportunity
- The relative size of the opportunity

> "I want this government not to fritter away its energies on all sorts of small schemes."
> —Winston S. Churchill

- A clear statement of the intended customers
- Likely profitability
- Competitive situation

Determining the Nature of the "Corporate Fit"

Although one should strive to be as quantitative as possible because it contributes to clarity, opportunity analysis is not all numbers, nor should it be. The importance of corporate culture in governing corporate capabilities was discussed in Chapter 5. Because different companies have different cultures, opportunities are not equally suitable for them.

In fact, an opportunity that is perfect for Company A may be totally unsuitable for Company B, even though the companies are the same size, in the same industry, and have similar resources available. The background, character, and history of the two enterprises may differ sufficiently that Company A could effect a spectacular success with the opportunity but Company B would simply be unable to capitalize on it. Company B may simply be too slow, too cautious, or find the opportunity inconsistent with deeply held values. There may be dozens of other reasons for the differences in capabilities. The point is, fitting the opportunity to the company is much more than a numbers game.

In addition to fitting well with a company's mission, goals, and strategies, opportunities should be analyzed to see if they make a good fit with the following:

- Areas of company competence
- Target market segments
- Cultural values and attitudes
- Available resources
- Corporate image
- Other intangible factors

- *Areas of Competence.* Much has been written in the past decade or so about areas of competence. A *core competence* is something the company does particularly well. The more specific the company is in defining and understanding its areas of particular competence, the more useful the information is to the opportunity analyst. A core competence may not be unique to the company in that competitors may possess the same competence—and more of it.

A *distinctive competence* is something the company does well and competitors do not do well. It is in this sense "unique" in the markets the company competes in. A distinctive competence is strategically more valuable than a core competence because it may be the source of relative superiority or relative competitive advantage.

- *Target Market Segments.* The importance of a clear view of customer targets is nowhere greater than in the evaluation of opportunities. One of the primary reasons for going to so much trouble to identify those strategic market segments where success is most possible is to permit concentrating corporate resources in precisely those areas and no others. If management finds itself seriously considering opportunities outside these carefully selected targets, it is either wasting its time now or wasted it when selecting targets.

Having such a clear market segment focus permits the organization to focus its energies in the chosen areas and not fritter away time and money fishing in a river with no fish. Proposals for pursuing opportunities outside the selected market targets should not be considered or even proposed.

- *Cultural Values.* It would be an unusual company in which the management and employees did not know which things just go against the grain. If at all possible, most organizations are better off avoiding areas in which employees and management must engage in activities for which, for whatever reason, they cannot generate enthusiasm.

The manufacturer of aircraft components that require extremely close tolerances and material specifications would be unlikely to find an opportunity to produce generic V-belt pulleys at the lowest price a great fit. The company almost certainly has invested years in training and developing, and the employees probably have a sense of pride in their skills and the products they make. It may be impossible for the employees to selectively lower their standards to produce a product they regard as beneath their skills and experience.

○ *Available Resources.* Underestimating—and hence underfunding—a carefully selected opportunity can be disastrous. Once committed, the company is faced with the unpleasant choice of abandoning the project, with all the negative implications of such a choice, or—and possibly worse if the project is really large—finding the additional resources necessary to continue. Companies have been forced into insolvency in precisely this manner.

What resources are required is not always clear-cut, particularly in those cases where company experience in that area is limited. Opportunities requiring new processes or new technologies should be examined with great care. Accordingly, cost estimates and personnel requirements should be budgeted with an eye to accommodating the inevitable setbacks along the way. This is a poor situation for applying unbridled optimism.

○ *Corporate Image.* Reputation is a powerful constraint in the marketplace. No company can move quickly to a new position on the competitive map, unless it is to a more lowly position. Potential customers will not accept a sudden move to a higher plane, regardless of its accuracy; nor will employees and suppliers.

A company's reputation is created as the result of its actions over many years. Because a long period of time is invested in creating the image, it will take a similar period to establish a new reputation. Certain automobiles have over the years come to be known for certain qualities, often unfavorable, such as weak electrical systems, or poor fit and finish, or always leaking oil. Such invective may still be heard today, despite the fact that the current quality level may be exemplary, and the reputed problem may have been cured years ago.

Any company deciding to build new products that represent a major departure from that which they are currently

> *It is better to underpromise than overcommit. The output will likely be the same; the results will be vastly different.*

known for may find the move more difficult than they may expect. We are not saying such a change may not be desirable, only that the effects of current or past reputation should be considered and addressed in the plan. The returns may come more slowly.

Analyzing and Selecting "Spontaneous" Opportunities

Not all opportunities, of course, are discovered in the proactive strategic manner advocated in this book. Ideas and discoveries often occur spontaneously in the normal course of business and deserve to be considered seriously. These ideas may be suggested by people in sales, design, engineering, or marketing—or by virtually anyone else inside or outside the company. The genesis of the idea or proposal is less relevant than the need to examine the proposal sincerely. A rigorous procedure for sorting and selecting such opportunities is important.

The purpose of the opportunity analysis and selection process for "spontaneous" opportunities is to ensure that the key strategic direction of the company would be better served by the proposed opportunity than it would by other opportunities also being proposed or pursued. The objective is no different from that proposed for the proactive process earlier in this chapter. Because these ideas by their very nature are outside the proactive process, however, they must be addressed somewhat differently.

Spontaneous opportunities are different insofar as they:

- Arise in an unpredictable manner.
- Usually must be addressed quickly because until they are, attention will be distracted from the current plan and direction.
- Are always tempting. They may look easy, or seem to represent a windfall, even though they actually detract from achieving the larger plan.
- Can cause ill-feelings if they have an internal constituency who may feel compelled to fight for pursuit of the appar-

ent windfall because they do not see the larger goal. Failing to explain the unwillingness to pursue an opportunity to its supporters is always a mistake.

The first requirement of a spontaneous opportunity selection process is that everyone involved understand the opportunity in precisely the same way. As with the proactive process, the spontaneous opportunity process is designed to be:

○ Market driven
○ Strategically focused
○ Pragmatically implemented

Figure 9-1 shows the key elements in a rigorous opportunity analysis, culminating in a correct decision for the organization in question.

Figure 9-1. The opportunity selection process.

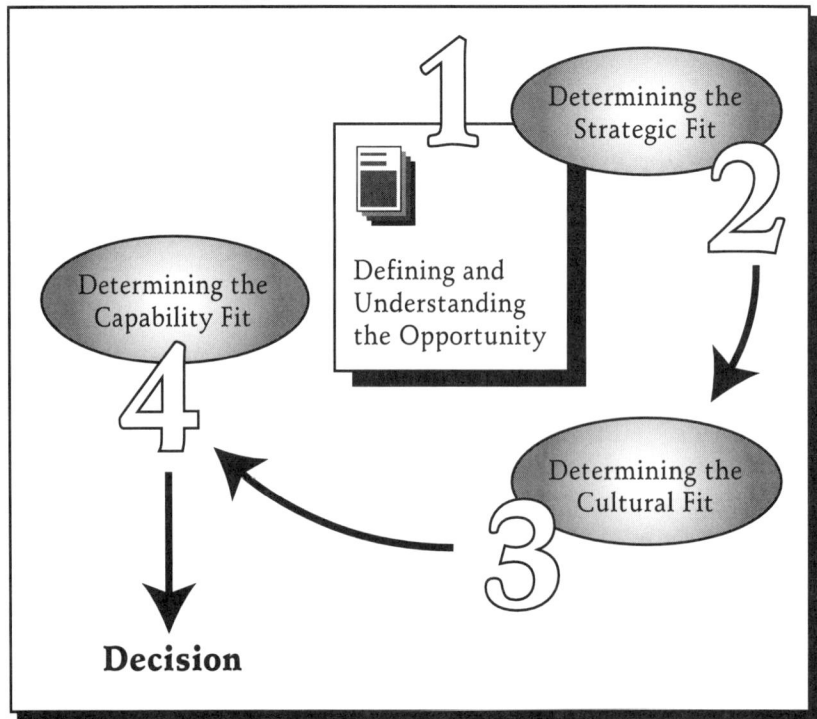

Conducting a Comprehensive Opportunity Analysis

Given the caveats regarding spontaneous opportunities and the tendency to let random ideas and opportunities distract management from its chosen strategy, we can move to a process for examining and selecting the best opportunities for your company to pursue. A comprehensive process will permit you to analyze either spontaneous or proactive opportunities. After all, the criteria for success is precisely the same in either case. Our opportunity analysis process, addresses strategic fit early to permit spontaneous opportunities to be dealt with quickly if they do not directly support the carefully developed corporate strategy. If judiciously followed, the proposed process will yield up opportunities that offer the greatest potential for success, and weed out those that are less desirable.

A rigorous, comprehensive opportunity analysis involves four key elements:

1. Defining and understanding the opportunity
2. Determining the strategic fit
3. Establishing the cultural fit
4. Determining the corporate capabilities fit

Defining and Understanding the Opportunity

The goal of opportunity analysis is to make a decision either to proceed or to terminate the investment of time and money in a given "opportunity." A clear and precise understanding of the opportunity is essential for any meaningful analysis. Although it may at first seem like a simple matter, often it becomes challenging to clearly define just what the opportunity is. Because the definition provides the base from which all ensuing steps derive, it is important to get it right. You must know and fully comprehend exactly what you are analyzing.

By looking at it from different perspectives, you can obtain a clear view of the opportunity. The simple exercises that follow are aids for examining various aspects of the new product opportunity so as to clearly understand it and its potential contribution to the strategic plan.

Categorizing the Opportunity

The following product categories are helpful for describing the opportunity.

- Physical product
- Intangible product
- Intellectual property
- Protectable idea (patent or copyright)
- A market opportunity
- An acquisition
- An alliance
- A start-up
- Other _____

The categories are not mutually exclusive—more than one may apply.

Identifying the Need

Perceived opportunities that do not satisfy a clear and significant need in the marketplace should probably be rejected. If it is difficult to state clearly what need is being served and for whom, the opportunity is problematic.

If, however, an opportunity might address needs not already being served by either your company or your competitors, it could be well worth considering. Unmet needs tend to be superior opportunities for premium return and sales growth. Try to identify any unmet need.

The two critical questions are these:

1. How is the need being satisfied now?
2. Why will this new way succeed?

A needs analysis worksheet is provided in Figure 9-2.

Determining the Source of Value

What is the "value" created by this opportunity? In this regard value accrues to two distinct groups. First, the customers derive

Figure 9-2. Analysis of need worksheet.

1. How is this need being satisfied today?

2. Is the present method inefficient? Ineffective? What can be improved?

3. What is good about the present method of satisfying the need?

4. Why will this new way be better and succeed?

5. What is the relative cost of the present method vs. the proposed method?

6. Is there an unmet need inherent in this opportunity? What is it?

value from the product or service, its availability, and its status. What parts do they value the most? What parts are less important?

Second, suppliers derive value from their participation in the ultimate sale. To get a clear picture of the value inherent in an opportunity, it is necessary to examine both sides of the equation. What do your suppliers value most?

What is the source of the value? Does the value emanate from some function being performed? Does it come from an economic benefit? Does the value come from availability, some special service, rapid delivery, or perhaps some innovative style or design? Whatever the source, it is important to understand its nature and qualities at the outset. It is easy for a project to proceed smoothly to conclusion with those involved having lost the real sense of value originally perceived. This can be effectively prevented only through a clear knowledge of the real source of value from the outset.

What does the value chain look like? A worksheet to help determine the source of value and the value chain is provided in Figure 9-3. Who gets the money? If the customer pays $1 for the product, how much of that is received by each of the players in the chain of delivery? How much do you get? How much do others such as retailers, wholesalers, parts suppliers, and all the others get? Does your company get enough to make the opportunity attractive? Would you redefine the opportunity based upon this value chain information?

Sizing the Opportunity

The sizing activity provides a basis for much if not most of the quantitative analysis for any new opportunity. Does the opportunity have international potential? North American potential? Domestic potential only?

The sales potential can vary immensely depending on the option chosen. Because the cost side of the equation is normally geared to the projected sales volume, sales projections are critical. If reliable published numbers do not exist (as for a completely new product or opportunity), assumptions will be necessary. When you use assumptions, it is prudent to clearly

Figure 9-3. Source of value worksheet.

1. What is the precise source of value to the purchaser/user? _____

2. What is the precise source of value to the producer/provider? _____

3. What is the anticipated product life cycle for this opportunity? _____

Describe or estimate the value chain for this opportunity. For this purpose, the value chain is defined as the total final cost paid by the purchaser allocated among all participants (producers, suppliers, etc.) financially benefiting in the delivery of the finished product or service.

Express as a bar chart totaling 100%.

label them and provide some background on how the projections were derived.

Extreme accuracy, however, is generally not required at this point. You need only be accurate enough to make the desired decision. If accurate data are available, so much the better, but it would be a waste of time to spend a great deal of time developing information of much greater precision than the decision demands. In most cases 80 percent accuracy is just fine. Following are the elements to consider:

Domestic Markets	*Global Markets*
○ Market potential	○ Market potential
○ Scope of application	○ Scope of application
○ Future potential	○ Future potential
○ Target market	○ Target market

A worksheet to help in sizing the opportunity is provided in Figure 9-4.

In cases where reasonable quantification is not possible, you may be able to create a series of logical statements that could guide research efforts to further clarify the size of the opportunity. What parameters seem reasonable?

To understand the opportunity it is important to ask, "Is there anything relative to the decision that we do not yet know?" What inherent aspects of the opportunity do we need to understand to make a good decision? These elements will tend to be qualitative rather than quantitative aspects of the opportunity. Here are some possibilities:

- ○ Corporate competencies required
- ○ Specialized skills—knowledge
- ○ People requirements—staffing
- ○ The economics of the sale of the product or service
- ○ Management requirements

Determining the Strategic Fit

The words *strategy* and *planning* are often used interchangeably, but in the strategic sense they are not the same. To apply the

Analyzing New Product Opportunities 141

Figure 9-4. Sizing the opportunity worksheet.

Estimate the total market potential for this opportunity. Use one or more situations.

Product or scenario	Year 1	Year 3	Year 5
A.			
B.			
C.			

Estimate the sales volume (to your company) for one or more likely situations.

Product or scenario	Year 1	Year 3	Year 5
A.			
B.			
C.			

1. What is the scope of this opportunity? _____

2. What future trends impact this opportunity? _____

3. Explain the target market assumptions governing the sizing analysis. _____

4. _____

principles of strategy you must differentiate between strategy and planning. *Strategy* refers to those activities directing competitive actions wherein an adversarial relationship is present. The primary weapons of strategy are sales, promotion, and customer service. Strategy offers principles for winning in competitive situations.

Planning refers to those activities directing actions that are essentially noncompetitive, such as a benefits plan, a financial plan, or a snow removal plan. Planning is a necessary and important tool for managing efficiently. However, many "plans" have nothing whatever to do with competing in the marketplace to win business, and hence the principles of strategy are not applicable to this kind of planning.

The Strategic Focus

In determining strategic fit, you are concerned primarily with the potential of the product or opportunity to compete effectively in a competitive and adversarial environment, specifically, one or more of the targeted market segments you have chosen to compete in. There are two fundamental questions to answer:

1. Does this opportunity directly support the strategic direction of the organization?
2. Is this product opportunity able to compete effectively in the marketplace? More precisely, can *you* compete effectively with this product? (The two issues are not always the same.)

The Competitive Environment

If the product will be competing globally as well as domestically, both environments must be considered. One might argue that the global environment cannot be ignored even if the product will compete only domestically. Choose a workable unit of measure for global considerations.

Domestic	*Global*
○ Key competitors	○ Key competitors
○ Competitive reaction	○ Competitive reaction
○ Competitor strengths	○ Competitor strengths

Analyzing New Product Opportunities

Will there be global impact on domestic sales potential, competitors or strategies? Will you cause an undesirable retaliation? Some opportunities are attractive only if they allow a company to become a major player in a relatively short time. In that case the ability to secure significant market power and influence may be a major consideration.

In determining the competitive environment, you also need to know your competitors' approach to doing business. What are the competitors' strategies? How do they do business? What is their competitive advantage? What do you know about how they conduct their business that would help you with the decision at hand?

Are the competitors for this opportunity familiar to you? If not, additional information is clearly warranted before taking on the new opportunity. Avoiding surprises is a good idea anytime, but when the investment is significant, it is highly imprudent to proceed with little knowledge of the primary competitors. A worksheet to help determine the competitive environment is provided in Figure 9-5.

Competitive Competencies

What are your present corporate strengths that will enable you to compete successfully in this opportunity area? What competitive resources (e.g., sales, promotion, service) do you bring to this opportunity? Do you possess strong market position? Why will you succeed where others have failed? (Figure 9-6 provides a worksheet to aid in examining your competitive competencies.)

Key Strategic Principles

One can spend a lifetime studying and mastering the art of strategy. We don't have nearly that long, but there are several strategic principles that have great bearing on the new product decision. These key concerns can be dealt with briefly and usefully at this time.

- Concentration of resources at the decisive point
- Relative versus absolute superiority

(text continues on page 146)

Figure 9-5. Competitive environment worksheet.

Define the general environment in which you will have to do business if you proceed with the proposed opportunity. Use additional space if necessary. Add any relevant topics not included.

1. Name the major competitors to be confronted in this opportunity. Rate competitive effectiveness of each: 1 = not at all, 10 = virtually invincible. _____

2. How competitive is the business environment? Presently? In the future? _____

3. What will be your source of competitive advantage? _____

4. Is the competitive advantage likely to be sustainable? For what period? _____

5. Competitor: _____
   Strategy
   Competitive strength _____

6. Competitor: _____
   Strategy
   Competitive strength _____

7. Competitor: _____
   Strategy
   Competitive strength _____

8. Competitor: _____
   Strategy
   Competitive strength _____

Figure 9-6. Competitive competencies worksheet.

Identify the important competencies (core competencies and distinctive competencies) that can be brought to bear on this opportunity. Describe how each competency will be employed. Add any relevant topics not included.

Competency	How Used?
1. _____	_____
2. _____	_____
3. _____	_____
4. _____	_____
5. _____	_____
6. _____	_____

- Offense versus defense
- Ordinary and "extraordinary" resources
- Clear statement of purpose
- Simplicity

Precisely why and how are you going to win? If you aren't sure, it's necessary to learn more about how the competitive environment is expected to unfold. Luck favors a prepared mind. A worksheet to help in examining strategic principles is provided in Figure 9-7.

Because opportunities that do not directly support the strategic direction of the company must be avoided, if your analysis thus far does not yield a good fit with the strategic direction of the company, then there is no need to proceed further with the analysis. Why spend the time and money if you already know the opportunity is a "no go"? If the opportunity does not directly support a key strategy, then it is not an opportunity. A worksheet is provided in Figure 9-8 as an aid in examining for strategic fit.

Establishing the Cultural Fit

If you determine that you have a good strategic fit with the direction of the company, it's time to move on to the second major area of consideration. After strategic fit, lack of cultural compatibility may be the leading reason for failures of new opportunities. As noted in Chapter 5, every company has a unique set of values and beliefs that provide for a smooth working relationship between employees. Large organizations may exhibit several distinct patterns of enculturation across various divisions or subsidiaries.

Opportunities that require activities or qualities that go against the prevailing culture will find it rough going. Opportunities demanding decisiveness and speed at every juncture find little support in organizations that pride themselves on conservative, contemplative management. The project will always seem to be "behind the curve."

To determine the cultural fit for a new opportunity, you

Analyzing New Product Opportunities

Figure 9-7. Competitive principles worksheet.

Note which strategic principles can be brought to bear on this competitive environment. Describe how the principle will be employed. Add any relevant principles not shown.

Strategic Principle	How Employed?
1. Absolute superiority	
2. Relative superiority	
3. Concentration of sufficient resources at the decisive point	
4. Ordinary and extraordinary resources	
5. Simplicity	
6. Surprise	

Figure 9-8. Strategic fit (mission-goals-strategies) worksheet.

The purpose of this worksheet is to relate the opportunity being considered to your corporate mission, goals, and strategies. The opportunity should be consistent with the established corporate direction.

Write in applicable	Check appropriate block
1. Mission Statement: _____ _____ _____	Clear and direct fit ☐ Unclear, possible fit ☐ Not covered in mission ☐ Does not fit ☐
2. Applicable goal or goals: _____ _____ _____	Clear and direct fit ☐ Unclear, possible fit ☐ Not covered in mission ☐ Does not fit ☐
3. Applicable strategy 1: _____ _____ _____	Clear and direct fit ☐ Unclear, possible fit ☐ Not covered in mission ☐ Does not fit ☐
4. Applicable strategy 2: _____ _____ _____	Clear and direct fit ☐ Unclear, possible fit ☐ Not covered in mission ☐ Does not fit ☐
5. Applicable strategy 3: _____ _____ _____	Clear and direct fit ☐ Unclear, possible fit ☐ Not covered in mission ☐ Does not fit ☐

NOTES: _____
_____
_____
_____
_____

should consider several dimensions, specifically those most relevant to your organization's ability to exploit the proposed activity. The dimensions selected for this analysis are as follows:

- Adaptive skills (adaptable versus inflexible)
- Strategic aptitude (strategically focused versus passive)
- Action orientation (decisiveness versus contemplative)
- Problem solving skills (innovation versus tradition)

Although not an exhaustive list, these four dimensions do permit you to develop a reasonable perspective on the ability to exploit a new opportunity. If the fit is poor, it may be wise to examine the requirements of the opportunity in much greater detail before proceeding blindly.

If the corporate fit between the culture and the opportunity is poor, it is generally better to pass in favor of an opportunity more consistent with the nature of your organization and personnel. If the opportunity fails the cultural fit test, you can stop here.

The Corporate Capabilities Fit

The consideration of specific capabilities is intentionally discussed last in this chapter. Most approaches for examining opportunities begin at this point. As noted, however, many opportunities fall within the specific capabilities outlined here but fail miserably in execution—for the reasons noted previously in this chapter. For this reason, a hierarchical process is presented here wherein the first two criteria (strategic fit and cultural fit) must be met before you even consider the myriad technical and financial considerations pertaining to the opportunity. The idea is to kick the defective ideas out early and at the least cost in analysis.

There is really little new to add to the consideration of corporate capabilities analysis; it is sufficient to list the primary considerations that must be satisfied. Each should be addressed in a rigorous and comprehensive manner:

Knowledge and Skill

- Management time and skill
- Technical knowledge and skill
- Experience in this business
- Availability of personnel

Financial Investment

- Initial investment
- Ongoing financial requirements

Physical Facilities and Equipment

- Production facilities
- Distribution facilities
- Administrative facilities

Technology

- Manufacturing technology
- Distribution technology
- Information technology

Distribution

- Current distribution channels
- New distribution channels

Promotion and Merchandising

- Skills availability
- Compatibility with existing image

Summary

Selecting the best opportunity, not just the next opportunity, is the moral of this chapter. Avoiding the temptation of the spontaneous idea or opportunity that does not directly contribute to the carefully chosen corporate strategy requires both judgment and vigilance.

A proactive approach to generating opportunities will help retain the focus necessary to achieve successful products in direct support of the corporate plan. The process proposed for analyzing opportunities will ensure that the company stays on track. It consists of four elements:

1. *A clear and precise definition of the opportunity.* A vague definition is a poor start.
2. *Ensuring the fit with corporate strategy.* Opportunities that do not directly support the chosen strategy are not opportunities. They are distractions.
3. *Ensuring fit with the corporate culture.* Every company will find some opportunities much harder to implement because of their values and beliefs.
4. *Ensuring availability of resources.* Stretching is okay, but don't bite off more than you can chew.

Most companies tend to leap right to the nuts and bolts of opportunity analysis when strategic and cultural fit are usually at least as germane to successful implementation.

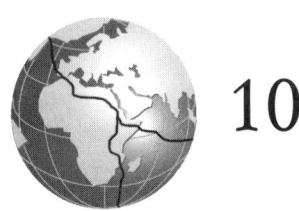

10

Planning the Proactive Product Development System: The Principles behind the Action

Why is it that so few new products succeed in the marketplace? One major reason is that the products do not meet the needs of the market nearly as well as do competitors' offerings. Companies need a product development system that provides a timely response to a perceived market need or opportunity. The system should be "repeatable," producing a similar product given an identical competitive context and a different product development team. This chapter and the two that follow discuss how to create such a new product development system.

The Design and Development Process

All organizations follow the same general path in designing and developing products. Following are the major steps in the process.

1. *Acquiring New Knowledge.* Innovative and successful new products generally require substantial new knowledge to be brought to market. Knowledge is needed in the following areas:

- *Field Intelligence.* This is knowledge about specific market segment needs and competitor actions and intentions.
- *Product Technologies.* A company may need to learn new technologies for developing some new products. Some of these technologies might be developed internally, but the majority will come from outside the company.
- *Process Technologies.* The company may need to learn about new manufacturing processes and about new ways of organizing manufacturing. Most of these advances will be made externally.

This knowledge base is not developed overnight and should not be thought about only when someone gets excited about a new product idea. Knowledge acquisition is a key strategic process, because there must be a specific strategic use for the knowledge. If corporate management does not insist on continual, strategically focused environmental scanning (continually searching for new and useful knowledge), the organization is doomed to long-run mediocrity.

2. *Needs Analysis.* Analyzing needs, discussed in Chapter 9, is the first step down the specific product development path after segment identification. At this point the company identifies a specific market need and confirms its basic capability to satisfy the need. The company must also make sure that it has a place for the product in its portfolio and that it needs the product (per the product plan). Executive management needs to be involved because it will need to be aware of the potential resource requirements—money, time, people, and capital equipment—to satisfy the need.

3. *Concept Investigation.* With executive management's approval in hand, the company can begin a detailed look at the product concept and start preparing the written design brief. To do this the company must obtain specific information on needs and expectations from the target market. It also needs to gather detailed information on competitive products and on regulatory and other constraints on the product and its use.

In some cases the product concept is straightforward. In others the best product concept may not be obvious at all but emerge only after considerable effort.

4. *Design Concept.* Armed with the specific details from the market and the regulatory environment, the company can translate these verbal inputs into a word picture of the product. Basic design is little more than a series of statements about the product in words and symbols understood inside the company. This is a technical step, carried out with pen and paper or some word processing package. Actually, it is probably more appropriate to think about basic *designs,* because in most cases there are several alternatives for satisfying the functional needs of the marketplace.

5. *Prototype Building.* Prototypes must be built for most products, both to test design the product in use and to get market feedback at the earliest appropriate times in the development process. Market feedback is very important, because product quality definitely has an aesthetic component, and users often can give good feedback only after using or handling the product. Prototyping also gives the company the chance to dynamically compare alternative designs, technologies, and materials.

6. *Pilot Production.* We would have difficulty mass producing many products that can be crafted by hand. We need to confirm our ability to produce the product once the basic design has been confirmed by prototyping. It is not unusual to find that we have to make minor changes to the product design detail in order to manufacture the product, but the changes should be few in number and very minor in nature.

7. *Manufacturing Ramp-Up.* The last step in the design and development process is the one involving the most people. New equipment and tooling may have to be purchased and installed (sometimes in new buildings). Materials must be sourced, people hired and trained, and support and information systems designed and installed. Then the manufacturing process has to be started up and gradually brought up to effective operating speed.

Often ignored in this process is the means of distributing products to customers and users. Product launch—a marketing responsibility—influences and in turn is influenced by manufacturing's ramp-up process and capabilities. This may involve beta testing, for example, or developing a priority sequence of customers, or simply stockpiling product until volume targets are met.

Design Problems

If the process steps are common, and the people involved are moderately intelligent, *why* does the process fail so often? Any process is only as strong as the weakest point, and problems created earlier in the design process can *never* be overcome by brilliant work at later stages. Where do these problems start?

We've already seen that there will most assuredly be problems if there is no strategic fit and if executive management is not involved. If executive management does not develop the overarching corporate strategy, does not approve the target segments, and does not approve the design concept, the product design team is really flying blind. We also know that we just don't get out of bed one morning and start the knowledge acquisition process. Furthermore, we know we have to be very careful, thorough, and objective about obtaining our market's real needs and expectations, just as we have to be careful, thorough, and objective about translating those needs and expectations into the basic product design. So why doesn't it happen?

Look in the mirror. If you are a marketer, how many times have your eyes glazed over when an engineer has made a presentation? If you are a designer, have you ever been smarter than the customer—or the manufacturing people? As a manufacturer, have you ever opted out of the development process, only to complain later when you couldn't meet cost and throughput objectives? As a player in the whole design and development process, have you ever wished the process were simpler?

The real problems with design are touched on in the preceding paragraphs. Good design comes as the result of a hard, detailed, time-consuming, and humbling process that requires

> *If the weak link fails, nothing makes subsequent effort effective.*

senior management involvement and the integration of knowledge and skills across the organization. It is not as simple as blithely filling in a few forms and passing them on to someone else.

We all know this, of course. Why, then, do we have problems? We have problems because we make the process unnecessarily complicated or don't have a detailed process that we can readily manage.

It's Not the Process—It's the People

Let's forget the process per se for the moment and think about what makes the process effective. In other words, let's think about the people in the process. Getting effective work out of good people requires:

- Commitment to the goal
- Enthusiasm
- Motivation
- Appropriate tools
- Appropriate knowledge and skills
- Good information
- Competence
- Integrated effort
- Good management systems

From a leadership point of view, we need to take competent, knowledgeable, and skilled people and have them work effectively. In the design process this effective work is likely to be in teams, groups, or gangs. Human beings are social animals and naturally congregate together. The challenge is to make the group an effective working team.

So we need commitment, motivation, enthusiasm, the appropriate tools, good information, good systems, and a means of integrating the effort. We are much more likely to get commitment and enthusiasm from people who want to be part of the process. People are positively reinforced by success and are motivated by a good challenge. Reward systems encourage individuals and groups to act so that they maximize their personal benefit. The greater the degree of process ownership, the greater the degree of commitment. The better the management systems, the more appropriate and timely the information available for use and the more likely that results will be appropriate.

Thus, the people *become* the process and vice versa. It is not possible to overstate the significance of the human element in successful product development. Every product and process decision ought to be taken with a conscious view to the specific people who will be doing the work.

The Proactive Product Planning System

To keep good people committed requires a product planning system that *works*. The authors have developed a system called the proactive product planning system, so named because it is a system, it is proactive, and it helps plan effectively for successful products. The system emphasizes these key elements:

- Executive management involvement
- Learning as a strategic objective
- Speed to market
- Experimentation—and a willingness to fail
- Rapid prototyping
- Dynamic and inclusive design and development teams

Executive Management Involvement

The easiest time to influence the outcome of the product development process is right up front; the most appropriate time for executive management to influence the process is right up front. New product decisions are critical strategic decisions in their own right, and executive management should be involved from the concept investigation stage. Yet we know executive management generally does not get involved in the process until prototypes are being built. Given a delay of months between concept investigation and prototype build, without a clear signal of executive management commitment, members of the development team may lose their enthusiasm.

From another strategic viewpoint, too, executive management involvement is critical. Any new product platform or system must be integrated into the company's total product portfolio. The only group with a clear strategic view is the executive management team. Designing new products and launching them ought to be relatively straightforward, and the product development team should be capable of performing that task. However, adding the new product without eliminating other products may add enough complexity to overload the manufacturing elements, which are still contending with the manufacture of the remainder of the company's products. Unless the impact on overall corporate performance is continually monitored—and only executive management can assess the impact—good outcomes from the process will be more or less coincidental.

Learning

Any company that wants to stay in business has to introduce new products at a regular rate. The development team, and the whole organization, should therefore be involved in capturing learning from each project. This is important for the individuals in the teams; learning is a personal activity, and each person should learn and develop during the project. If the company explicitly values such learning, the individual's sense of self-worth will increase—an important motivating factor and one leading to increased commitment. When the reward system reinforces the importance of learning, motivation and commitment increase. And because some of the learning is tacit, individuals develop a greater sense of ownership of their portion of the process and become more involved in it.

From the individual's perspective, any learning will be valued. From the company's perspective, though, the learning has to foster development capability, or else the value will be limited. Here are some areas in which attention should be strategically concentrated:

> *Ownership is key to commitment.*

- Procedures to be followed in the development process, including the capture and institutionalization of learning
- Tools and methods
- The process of development itself, including the transition from one project to the next
- The organizational structures used to operationalize the process
- The principles, ideas, and values that guide decisions in the process

According to Steven C. Wheelwright and Kim B. Clark, there are four approaches to building development capability:[1]

1. *Creating an Overarching Development Strategy.* This is most appropriate where there are series of complex, changing product lines, many project opportunities exist, and there has been (or is expected to be) an increase in development requirements.
2. *Changing the Development Process.* This approach works best where the firm is large, has a complex product line, and is functionally organized with a history of sequential (and independent) development.
3. *Creating "Building Block" Skills and Tools.* Smaller companies, or smaller project groups in larger organizations, with a history of teamwork benefit most from this approach.
4. *Setting Up Development Projects.* This approach can work well where well-defined technological or market opportunities exist. It is also appropriate when there is a clear demand or need for significant development improvement to ensure project success.

These four approaches can all work at the same time. What is needed is a clearly articulated learning and development strategy, along with the measurement metrics to monitor progress. Managers manage only what they can measure; subordinates perform to maximize personal benefit. Reward systems need to be structured to encourage behaviors that are in the company's best interests—which will generally happen only when they are in the employee's best interests as well.

Speed to Market

First in is best dressed. The early bird gets the worm. Early to bed and early to rise, makes a man healthy, wealthy, and wise. In other words, first in cleans up. This is becoming truer with the steady shortening of product life cycles. To get to market quickly with an appropriate product, the development system must have the following:

- A clear development target based on an identified target customer
- Clear business objectives
- A staff of competent people who have the conviction to remain committed under difficult circumstances
- An appropriate budget and support for the team
- A reward system that encourages quick decision making

Note that getting to market quickly by beating aggressive timelines is rewarding in itself, and it shortens the period of intensity. Who suffers more in a marathon—the person who runs the distance in 2.5 hours, or the person who runs the distance in 4 hours? Who suffers longer? Same distance, same goal, but one has a better plan, and better capability. And may run more marathons.

There is plenty of evidence demonstrating the strategic importance of speed to market. General Motors and Honda announced the launch of Saturn and Acura, respectively, in the same month, with market presence scheduled for the same year. Honda was on time; General Motors was so late that Acura had been through three model changes by the time Saturn rolled off the assembly line. Honda's development process involved developing a new vehicle for an established manufacturing system and environment; GM's development process involved a complete change in philosophy as well as a complete change in everything related to design and manufacture of a vehicle. GM bit off much more than it could chew. Given the complexity of the challenge and the great number of projects spread over limited resources (a fairly common phenomenon in design groups), however, the time to market was actually quite reasonable. But it was a very long time. And over time the environment and expectations changed.

When the first Saturn was purchased in 1990, it was an eight-year-old design. The 1990 Acura was, at most, a two-year-old design—and with many customer suggestions designed into the new model. Given the shift in competitor-driven market taste and needs, which vehicle is more likely to meet market acceptance? Where tastes shift and evolve, speed to market is essential to capture more of the current taste.

BMW tends to make its model changes in four-year cycles, with major technological changes incorporated in the new model. Acura makes more frequent model changes and is always introducing incremental changes each year. Which is more in tune with the North American market, the market both companies see as the most important for them in the next few years? Given the growth in sales, probably Acura. In established products smaller, more frequent changes tend to be more easily incorporated into existing manufacturing processes and distribution channels than major changes.

Experimentation

Experimentation—*focused* experimentation—is an important part of the product development process. The only essential components of any experiment are a hypothesis or an idea to test and an absolute willingness to accept that the idea could have no value. At the strategic level, a commitment to experimentation early in the process—at the time of concept investigation—will identify product concepts that should not be allowed to go forward into design. If executive management insists on appropriate experimentation and commits to acting according to the results of the experiments, the company will conserve resources and save the financial and time costs associated with failed products.

Too often, experimentation is done too late in the development process because most managers think of experiments in terms of physical market tests of products or laboratory experiments on physical characteristics. This is too limiting; much experimentation can be undertaken before any physical experiments could possibly be conducted. In fact, properly designed and conducted focus groups—using the appropriate audience—are among the most powerful experiments companies conduct. Market inquiry is powerful because, if it's not done right, nothing that follows will be more than coincidentally appropriate.

Computer-based simulation software now makes experimenting with corporate strategy and changes to the strategy a reality. One of the most powerful uses of simulation lies in testing the overall impact of a new product on the organization. This testing should not be limited to looking at the cannibalization effects on existing products; it is even more critical to simulate the impact of the new product design on existing and alternative manufacturing processes and systems. This might show up aspects of the product that would mess up the ability to control costs and deliver on volume, which would only jeopardize a company's ability to retain desired customers—and to meet overall sales and profit objectives.

Many managers are unable to internalize "sunk cost" and treat physical experiments simply as modification trials (even if the outcome is an unequivocal rejection), not as fundamental "abandon or continue" decision points. The later in the process the experiments are conducted, the less likely the organization is to stop development. Managers argue that too much has been invested and that, for a small amount more in development funds, a product can be got into the marketplace, where sales can be made to help recover some of the development investment. So instead of abandoning the turkey, the company adds more money and more time to the project, reinforcing failure.

All of the experiments do not have to be conducted in-house. Often, beta test sites allow testing of various options before the product is taken to market. The greater the degree of uncertainty, the greater the number of variants that should be tested. Often, this is the only way to experiment with the form of the product, even when you are happy with the function.

Rapid Prototyping

Prototypes are an important form of experiment. From a strategic point of view, they are most effective when used to test one or two hypotheses and when the time from prototype testing to usable knowledge development is short. This may mean more prototype testing cycles rather than fewer. Traditionally, prototypes have been the province of engineers and have been very much a technical tool, useful only to the initiated. They ought to become a powerful management tool used to influence the whole development process.

One key strategic concern with prototypes is the involvement of customers, which depends on the role that managers see for customers in the development process. As a general rule, the more incremental the development, the earlier in the process customers should be involved, because customers can really talk about only what they already know and are most emphatic about issues or attributes that annoy them. It is no surprise that when asked about in-flight service, airline passengers immediately complain about the food and seats.

There are few hard-and-fast rules for selecting key customers. Two groups should always be represented, though: demanding customers and opinion leaders. Demanding customers need not be inveterate complainers; in fact, they probably aren't. But we are all familiar with customers who quietly but firmly insist on getting what they want (or were promised) and who know what is achievable—and how. We are all familiar, too, with key accounts that influence the majority by their early adoption of a new product. United Airlines and British Airways were seen early as critical to the success of the Boeing 777, and their announcement of purchases led other airlines to purchase the aircraft well before the first flight.

Design Teams

One of the most critical development decisions is choosing the development team and deciding where the design process should take place.

The larger and more geographically dispersed the organization, the more difficult this decision is to make. As a general rule, the more technology-driven the development and the greater the cross-divisional applicability of the product or the technology, the more appropriate it is to locate the design team in or close to corporate headquarters. The more market-driven the product and the lower the likelihood of interdivisional transfer, the more appropriate it is to locate the design team close to the key market segment. Either way, it is always highly desirable to have customer involvement in the design process.

Summary

In this chapter, we've looked at the elements of the basic product development process, and at the keys to success of an effective product planning system. We've introduced the name of the system we believe is the most appropriate system to use: the proactive product development system. In the next three chapters, we will describe the system, and discuss how to use the system effectively to place powerful products into production, and into the hands of delighted customers.

Note

1. Steven C. Wheelwright and Kim B. Clark, *Revolutionizing Product Development* (New York: The Free Press, 1992), pp. 312–323.

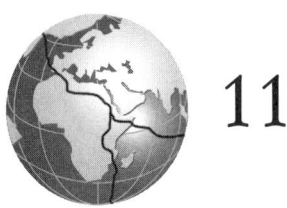

11

Creating the Proactive Product Development System

What would happen if you had a new product development process that was easy to use and that was repeatable each time, no matter which representative group was involved in the process? You would have a constant stream of successful products and would be continually looking for more manufacturing resources to cater to the increasing demands from our target market segments.

Fortunately, such a process exists. Introduced in Chapter 10, it is called the proactive product development system. It works because it is simple to use, because it automatically includes active input from all interest groups, and because it is sensitive to corporate culture and the culture of the market segment. This chapter is devoted to a description of the system in use and also discusses the people that drive the process—the new product project team, particularly the team leader.

Propositions

The proactive product development system is based on three key propositions:

1. The market segment for which the product is to be developed is known.
2. The company's senior executives confirm the strategic fit of the product concept.
3. The company wants to produce something that will capture a preestablished share of the market.

If all three of these propositions are satisfied, the critical work is already done. The rest is mere detail! We all know, of course, that the devil is in the detail. There is a lot of hard work to be done before the product enters service with the first customer.

The Model

The proactive product development system, shown in Figure 11-1, has four basic stages:

1. *Strategic.* This stage is where you confirm that all the important strategic prerequisites have been satisfied before you devote time, resources, and energy to developing a specific product. These prerequisites have been discussed earlier in the book.
2. *Concept Design.* This is where you use the knowledge gained during the strategic stage to produce the design brief for the product. Armed with the design brief, you can now hear from the market what it wants and needs, and how it expects to be satisfied. You also gain insights from other important "customer" groups, such as your own engineers and independent distributors. Using this knowledge, you now develop the product concept, which should be endorsed by your senior management before proceeding to the next stage. If you have not done so before, this is where you also research competitors' products to determine how well each of them satisfies the target market.
3. *Detailed Design.* Here you develop the detailed product specifications and finalize the design of the processes by

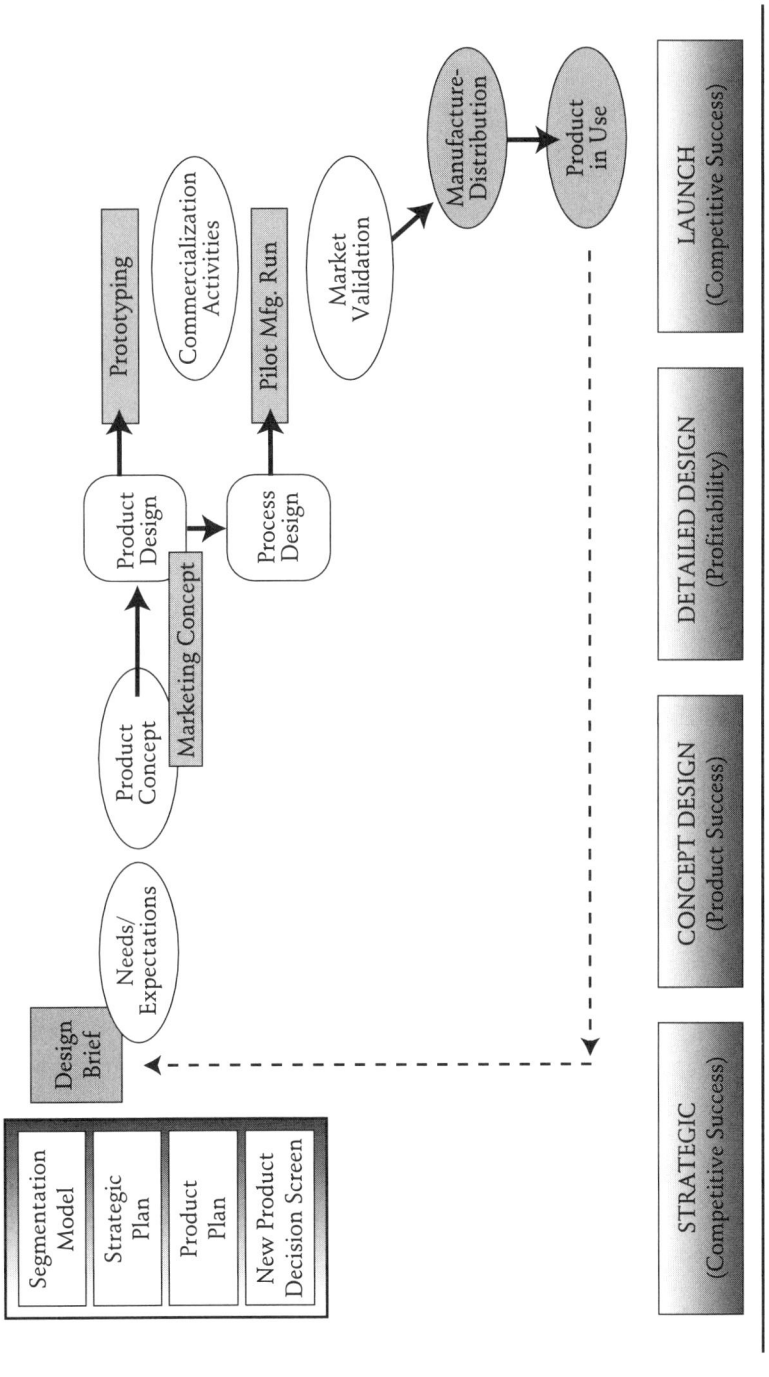

Figure 11-1. The proactive product development system.

which the product will be manufactured and placed in the hands of the customers. During this stage, you might use prototypes and pilot manufacturing runs to validate the appropriateness of the product as designed.
4. *Launch.* At last, it's time to ramp up production, get the product to market, and confidently await the rush of orders as your customers acknowledge that you gave them what they wanted.

Concept Design

Customers have ideas about what a product should do—what functions they want the product to provide, or the uses to which it can be put. You don't want to limit yourself to the "product in use," however, or else you will ignore important groups that also have vested interests in the purchase process. Rather, you need to think about the *modes* of use. Typical modes are manufacture, distribution, transportation, storage, installation, use, maintenance, repair, and retirement. To this can be added activities that involve the product in nontangible ways. These include specifying, ordering, and managing the application and utilization of the product. The number of interested groups has suddenly increased dramatically.

So you need to understand what the needs and expectations of each important set of customers is. To do this you have to work with the customers. This takes time, skill, and attention to detail. It is worth doing well.

You need to determine what the various constituencies need in the product—the product's *functions*—and their expectations of how those needs will be satisfied—the *services* that support the product over its service life and the manner in which those services will be provided. You also need to determine (1) the

> *Product design is made easier by knowing what the key market segment wants.*

relative importance of each of those needs and expectations, (2) how well competitors' products rate on each of these attributes, (3) how well your *current* products rate on each of these attributes, and (4) how well any new product will have to rate in order for a particular attribute to be an order winner.

As previously noted, this is an important and time-consuming task; it is one of the most important operational tasks the marketing people undertake. But you can simplify it. You can rely on three characteristics of human nature to simplify right at the beginning:

1. The inability to think in multidimensional space (i.e., not being able to think effectively about more than three different things at one time)
2. The inability to make calculated judgments about that which we don't know or have not experienced
3. The inability to express ideas and concepts clearly and unequivocally

The implications of these characteristics are profound. No matter how effective you *think* you have been in gathering information from customers, only *prototypes* will provide you—via your customers—with really effective feedback. The further the leap into the unknown with the new product, the more urgent the need for *rapid* prototyping.

Preparing the Design Brief

Before you can obtain information from the customer groups, you must first prepare the design brief. This requires you to:

1. Describe the product
2. Identify the "product construct envelope"

Describing the Product

The product should be described in a single sentence, capturing the essence of what is desired in word pictures understood by everyone involved in the development of the product. Here are two examples:

Write a book on product development for senior and midlevel executives.

Design a commuter aircraft capable of carrying fifty passengers over distances of up to 1,000 miles.

Honda, when developing the Accord, defined the project as *"designing a car for a rugby player."* The symbolism was powerful, succinct, and universally understood within the company. Symbols and metaphors allow us to capture the essence of the product in a very brief statement that people can remember.

Identifying the Product Construct Envelope

After developing a working definition of the product, you need to produce a "product construct envelope," a list of statements about requirements concerning product performance, including product cost. There are three types of requirements:

1. *Absolutes.* These requirements *must* be satisfied, and the statement must contain a "must" clause.
2. *Ideals.* These requirements *should* be satisfied, but failure to satisfy an issue is not fatal.
3. *Desirables.* These requirements *ought to* be satisfied, but they will *always* be traded off in favor of a more critical requirement where necessary.

As with the product definition, you should first make a brief statement about the requirement, ideally as a one- or two-word heading. This is followed with a brief description of a perspective on the requirement, supported by background information that is comprehensive enough and detailed enough to provide a nontechnical briefing to an interested reader. This background information should include an analysis of how competitors have handled the same issue and what developments are likely in relevant technologies. It is likely that you will have more than one perspective on a requirement; you develop as many statements as there are perspectives.

Using the book example, you might come up with a requirement like this for physical dimensions:

Issue. Physical dimensions.

Perspective. The book *must* contain fewer than 300 pages.

Background. Competitive books contain between 150 and 180 pages of text. These books are slim enough to fit in an executive attaché case and compact enough to be read on aircraft. Slim volumes are also associated with higher-level strategic thinking (thicker volumes are associated with more technical writing) in published perception studies. None of the competitive books addresses issues critical to senior executives as well as issues critical to marketing *and* manufacturing executives, which implies this book may contain more words than does the competition.

This list of statements constitutes the construct envelope for the product. The list, and the background that is developed for each perspective, is not the "property" of the designers. This information is first used by market researchers to check the validity of the assumptions as the process of identifying customer demands is carried out. It is vital that you test these assumptions about the perspectives.

Identifying Customer Needs and Expectations

With the product defined and the product construct envelope determined, you can now work with customers to identify what each group wants and needs in the product in terms that are clear enough to be understood by most people. This condition is very important; if, after having worked with customers, people inside the company do not understand clearly and accurately what customers actually want, the chances that the product will satisfy the customers are greatly reduced. You have to gather what has been described as "the voice of the customer" in unambiguous terms.

You can do this by recording customer needs and expectations as brief statements. These can be augmented with information from other sources—warranty claims, trade journal articles, complaints, and direct and indirect observation of customers using the products. You might record some customer needs in the following way:

Book short chapters
 easy to read
 comprehensive bibliography

Aircraft use gravel airstrips
 walk down aisle without stooping
 low fuel consumption

You also need to find out how important each one of these needs and expectations is for your customers. You find out by talking with your various customer groups, and by using internal and external marketing experts. You then record all this in a "customer need/product characteristic matrix," as shown in Figure 11-2.

Figure 11-2 introduces a new product: a chocolate chip cookie. The authors each have different preferences in chocolate chip cookies, and these preferences are probably different from yours. Personal preferences aside, though, you have to develop a product the market wants, so you use market research to determine what the customer needs and expectations are, and the relative importance the target market segment places on each need. These needs form the rows in the matrix.

Your research shows that there are eight important needs, with varying levels of importance to the customer. An importance level of 5 means absolutely essential; an importance level of 1 means minor importance. You will use the importance level after filling in the matrix.

A critical element in the matrix is the list of attributes that forms the columns in the matrix. Most of these attributes are product characteristics that you, the manufacturer, control. Individually, they influence one or more customer demands. These product characteristics need to be controlled to ensure that the customer demands are met.

For the customer need "no broken cookies," you control cookie thickness, cookie diameter, cookie hardness, and packaging (and other elements not mentioned). For the customer need

Creating the Proactive Product Development System 175

Figure 11-2. The customer need/product characteristic matrix.

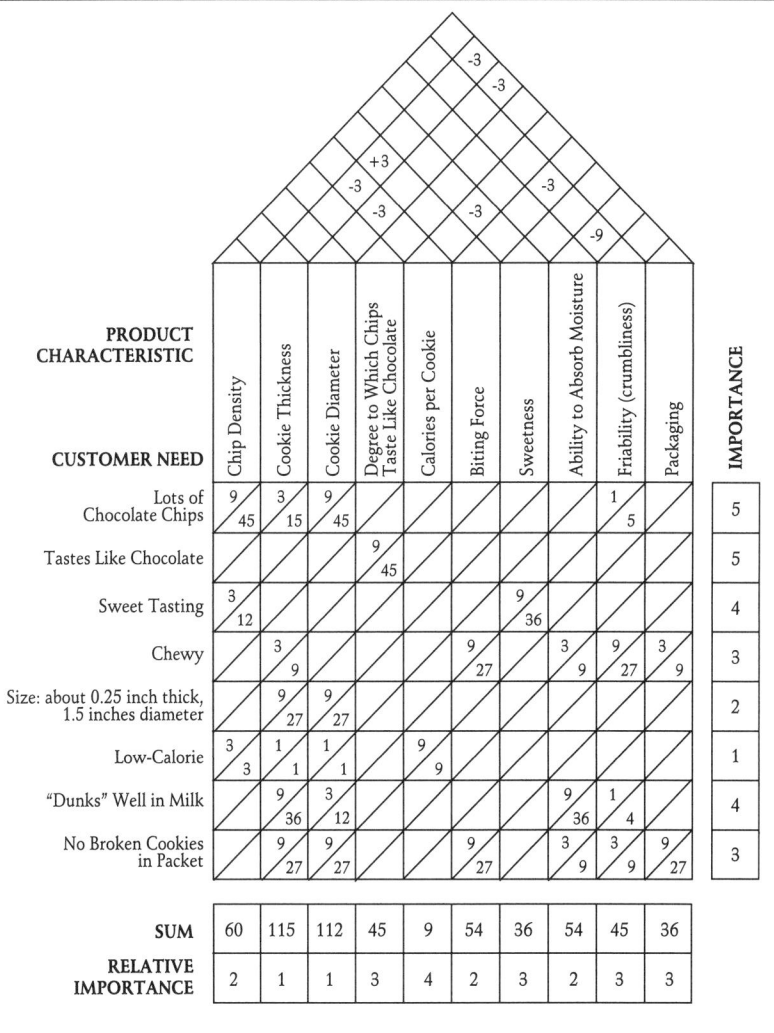

Product Characteristic Interaction Matrix: Legend

High Positive Interaction: +9
Some Positive Interaction: +3
Some Negative Interaction: -3
High Negative Interaction: -9

"tastes like chocolate," you control the degree to which the chips taste like chocolate, and the sweetness level of the cookie. You record the characteristics you control as column headings in the matrix.

After identifying all the product characteristics that influence your ability to satisfy all the customer needs and expectations, you can begin to determine which are the most important controllable product elements.

Filling in the Matrix

Using the matrix of customer needs and controllable characteristics, you look at each cell in turn and determine how much impact the particular characteristic has on satisfying the particular customer need. This is the "relationship score," graded on the following scale:

- *Strong*, 9
- *Moderate*, 3
- *Possible*, 1
- *Zero*, the cell is left empty

You enter the relationship score in the upper half of the cell.

Next, modify the relationship score by the importance the customers and the market attach to the particular demand (which you determined from your market research) by multiplying the relationship score by the degree of importance customers attach to the particular need. You enter this modified score in the lower half of the cell.

How important is the characteristic "chip density"? Chip density has a strong relationship with the customer need "lots of chocolate chips," which has a market importance of 5. You enter the relationship score of 9 in the upper half of the "lots of chocolate chips/chip density" cell, and the modified score of 45

> *Identify and concentrate on the significant few, not the trivial many.*

(the product of the market importance of the customer need and the relationship score) in the lower half of the cell. Chip density has a moderate relationship with "sweet-tasting," which has a market importance of 4; you enter the numbers 3 and 12 in the appropriate sections of the cell. The other customer need that is influenced by chip density is "low calorie"; the relationship is moderate (3) and, with a market importance of 1, the modified score is 3. You add the modified scores for all the cells in the column together, and arrive at a column score of 60 (45 + 12 + 3).

You do this for each column, and complete the matrix. The greater the total score for a column, the greater its overall influence on satisfying customer needs and expectations. By inspection, you can arbitrarily group product characteristics into clusters of their relative importance in satisfying customer needs. In Figure 11-2, cookie thickness and cookie diameter are the most important product characteristics.

Identifying Product Functions

One thing manufacturers know is that customers don't know everything about what functions a product should fulfill. What you need to do, therefore, is identify the various use modes and functions the product must fulfill. For the chocolate chip cookie example, the use modes are storage, shipping, retail display, and eating. Although the identification of the most critical product characteristics from the analysis of customer needs is critical, it is not necessarily sufficient. You also have to determine the relationship of the product characteristics with the list of functions you identified. You may have to add new product characteristics to be able to complete the analysis. "Retail display," for example, might require you to add a new characteristic, "shelf life," which might also influence "storage."

Having identified the product characteristics and used them with the customer need items and the internally generated product functions, you need to identify the interactions among all the product characteristics. Systematically identifying the correlations among product characteristics ensures that the designers do not forget these interactions—and forgetting them is a major

> *Knowing which characteristics influence each other helps immensely with managing design team coordination and integration.*

problem in effective design. Using the chocolate chip cookie example, you might reasonably expect to find a strong interaction between "cookie size" and "calories per cookie," and a strong interaction between "cookie thickness" and "biting force." Are these interactions positive or negative though? Interactions between pairs of product characteristics are positive if a change in one of the characteristics that enhances/detracts from market perception of the product produces a change in the other characteristic that would also enhance/detract from market perception. Interactions are negative when a "market-positive" change in one characteristic induces a "market-negative" change in the other characteristic. In a calorie-conscious world, you might decide from your market research that increasing calories per cookie would be market-negative, while a modest increase in cookie size would be market-positive; you might further decide that slightly thicker cookies and a modest increase in biting force are both market-positive.

In Figure 11-2, a matrix has been installed above the product characteristics. The individual interactions among pairs of characteristics have been inserted using numbers to indicate the degree and direction of the interaction. This will allow you to see at a glance which are the most significant interactions, and how to use them to influence the product development process.

When interactions are positive, it may be possible for you to eliminate a product characteristic from the matrix. When interactions are negative, the product characteristics are not compatible, and R&D or other creativity methods will be needed to resolve the incompatibilities. If the incompatibilities cannot be resolved, trade-offs will be needed—usually in favor of the more important of the pair of characteristics. Even if you decide to do nothing to resolve or modify interactions at this stage, knowing which are the critical interactions will help determine the organization of the product development, and lets individual designers or design teams know which others they should contact for design feedback.

A Pause for Reflection

Thus far you have defined the product, developed the product construct envelope, identified customer needs, and identified product functions. You have investigated how well competitors' products perform in the target marketplace. More important, you have identified the "market critical" customer needs and a more complete list of important product functions than your customers can articulate. You have also identified the correlations among the product characteristics.

Now you have enough good information to design an effective product. You have to first package the information so that it makes good sense and allows for the best use of all the available information. So you must think through what you need to do with the information.

As shown in Figure 11-3, we design products from the outside in and build them from the inside out. You need to go from the product level down through major systems, assemblies, subassemblies, components, and finally parts. You have to design not simply for intended use but also for manufacture, transportation, storage, assembly, maintenance, repair, and retirement. You have to design each of the elements at each of the five or six product levels and decide at the parts level what manufacturing technologies to use, what raw materials to use, and exactly how you will make the part. For higher levels you need to determine what transformation or assembly technologies to use as you assemble components and items that become increasingly complex and complicated.

It is human nature to jump to conclusions—to go through knee-jerk reaction without passing through disciplined thinking and research. The proactive product development system aims to eliminate that leap into the dark and replace it with deliberate thought. That does not mean becoming a slave to linear thinking. To the contrary, we need to be able to experiment, research, and investigate, and that means developing hypotheses about possi-

Figure 11-3. Product design and manufacture.

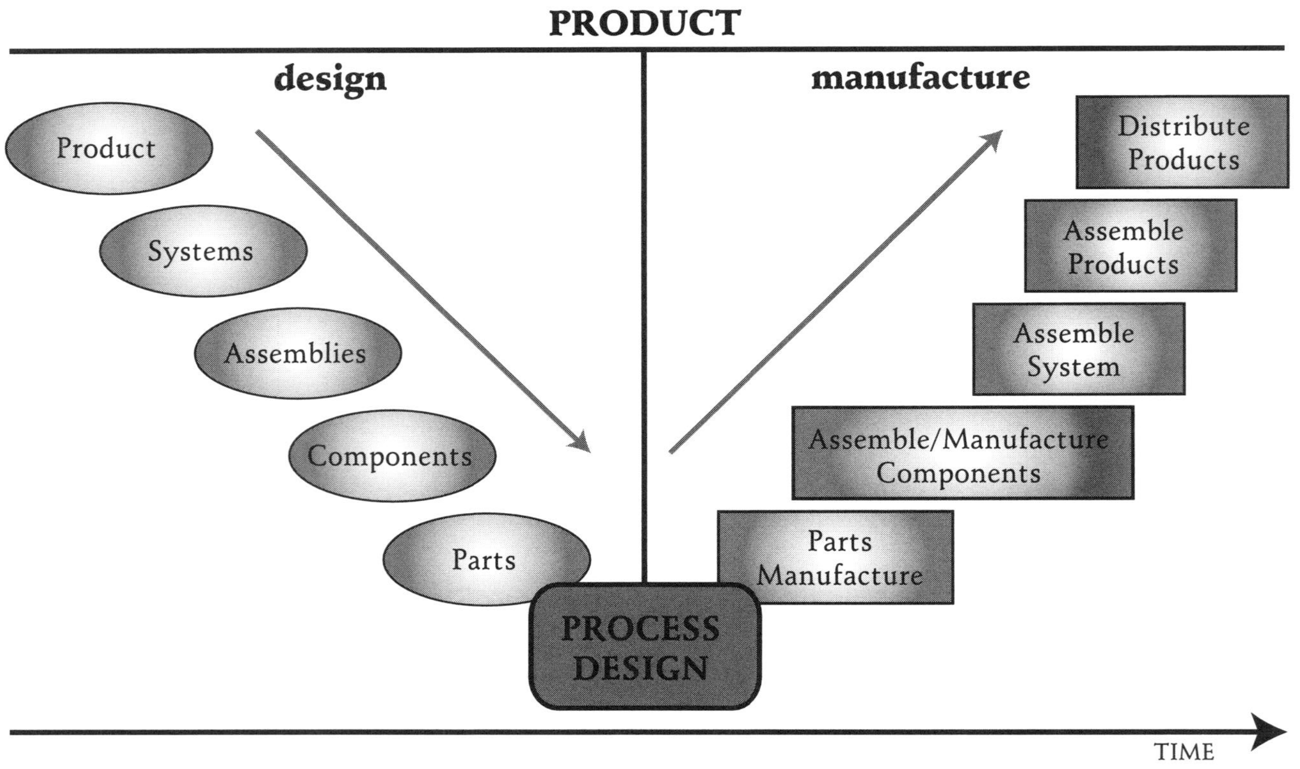

> *Higher-level decisions will constrain lower-level design.*

ble solutions to problems and issues and alternative ways of thinking.

Technology Decisions

You cannot design systems and parts without thinking about technology alternatives. You will think about and possibly hypothesize about alternatives as you design "from the outside in." You should not make any technology decisions, however, until you finalize the design of individual parts. The final design of the parts will influence the choice of technologies for handling and physically combining the parts and assemblies as you build up the product "from the inside out."

There are two basic forms of technology to be concerned with: (1) technologies embedded in the product and (2) manufacturing or other processing technologies.

Product Technology

New technologies embedded in new products are always a possibility and invariably appear to be attractive design options. This is especially true where there are obvious and immediate performance advantages for the purchaser and user of the new product. There are, though, several issues the design team needs to think through before new technology replaces old but good technology in a product:

- *Obsolescence.* Will the new technology make the technology in your other products obsolete if you introduce it now? If so, what would be the effect on purchase decisions (for the products)?
- *Internal Impact.* Will the new technology require major changes to the skills, knowledge, and organization of

companies purchasing the product? What would be the effect on purchase decisions?
- *Technology Support Net.* Do you have the infrastructure to support the new technology effectively? Does this support exist in your target markets? What would be the effect on purchase decisions?
- *Product Performance.* Will the new technology enhance current performance? Will the new technology increase the number of uses for the product? What would be the effect on purchase decisions?
- *Compatibility.* Will the new technology be compatible with technologies currently in use in the target companies? What would be the effect on purchase decisions?
- *Future Products.* Will the new technology provide a platform from which to launch more members in a new product family? What would be the effect on purchase decisions?
- *Future Features.* Will the new technology allow you to introduce new features to this product in the future? Can those potential uses be embedded now? What would be the effect on purchase decisions?

You need to develop effective research strategies to provide the information needed to address these issues effectively. Fortunately, embedded technology questions can be answered quite quickly, regardless of whether or not you have developed the technology. If you follow the lead of others, you can expect knowledgeable responses to the questions you ask customers. If you have already developed the technology, you can design experiments and build prototypes that will not only enable you to test the effectiveness of the technology but also allow you to gain good market insight. In both cases you have to identify the companies that will best be able to help in obtaining this information.

The issues are harder to address and surface if you are concerned with service aspects of the product. Because services (or intangible elements of the product) are becoming more dominant as order winners in both retail and industrial markets, the importance of researching and experimenting with the service components of the package cannot be overstated.

It is critical to realize that the interactions among service and tangible components of the product are every bit as important as the interactions among the tangible elements themselves. Also, despite the apparent ease with which service components should be able to be copied, it is obvious that firms can make service *the* critical competitive weapon—and sustain that competitive edge.

Process Technology

The strategic and operational questions the design team needs to ask about process technology changes should all be answered within the firm. It is important, though, that the right questions be asked. Questions arise in the following contexts:

- *Fit.* Does the potential new technology fit with the other processes used to manufacture the component under consideration? This involves consideration of scale and volume issues, as well as physical size and the ability to site the new equipment in a logical way without incurring great expense. In manufacturing plants where the layout and process flow seems tortuous, the cause is more often than not a result of "shoehorning in" replacement technology—at great longer-term cost to the company.
- *Skills and Knowledge.* Does the potential new technology fit with the skills and knowledge base and with the social organization of the company? If not, the consequences of adopting the new technology can be quite severe.
- *Utilization.* How fully will the new technology be used on this product if it is adopted? Overoptimistic estimates of capacity utilization for new technology often result in great pain for the company. Often, finding work to keep machines or people occupied takes priority over more competitively relevant issues; the outcome of this doesn't need to be guessed at.

Invariably, the process technology has an impact on product design, because the components are in a very real sense a derivative of the process by which they are made. Nonfamiliarity with new processes (or new materials) can lead to problems of market acceptance of the product in use. Where new process technologies are chosen, the company needs to consider prototyping for customer feedback and acceptance.

Design for Manufacturability and Assembly

It is a truism that quality cannot be built into a product; it is also true that functionality cannot be built into a product. Everything must be *designed* into the product, which means it has to be designed into the product's constituent parts. In addition to these considerations, it helps if the product is designed for easy and effective manufacture and assembly.

This book is not the place for a lengthy discourse on design for manufacturability and assembly (DFMA). It cannot be overemphasized, however, that DFMA is vitally important, even if customers are not aware of the concept, and you must have engineers and designers who are competent in the use of various DFMA techniques.

The concept of "design for . . ." also needs to be extended. DFMA almost automatically incorporates design for *disassembly* and maintenance, because that which goes together easily and quickly should also come apart simply and effortlessly. But we also need to think about design for component recovery and design for recycling at the end of the useful life of the product. When you think about these extensions, it is important to involve critical customers in thinking through which of these is important in the marketplace. Although trend analysis is helpful in trying to determine what the competitive environment will be like at the time the product is taken out of service, the reality is that the product will be purchased using assumptions held by the current purchasing decision makers. It may be bad short-term business to increase costs for a product all of whose utilities may not be appreciated by the marketplace. Of course, it may be good medium- and longer-term benefit to incorporate product elements that appear certain to be of interest to the marketplace in the future. These strategic design issues need to be addressed by senior executives, and not resolved by the design team acting alone.

Ironically, as more use is made of advanced automation in manufacturing, there is more need to pay attention to design for manufacturability and assembly. Machines are not as adept as people at recognizing and correcting the mistakes made by others; machines will either recognize the error condition and shut down or not recognize the error condition and compound the problem. Why did so many companies have to wait until they adopted advanced automation to design products that people could actually build?

Product Cost

Given everything else about the product, you have to ensure that the product manufacturing and distribution costs are such that you can profit from meeting the anticipated market demand. This generally means determining an acceptable market price, then an acceptable total cost for the product, and then working through what it will actually cost to get the product to the customer.

One logical means of determining costs is by using the *target costing* philosophy. This requires the design team to:

- Determine the maximum acceptable cost for the product.
- Determine the relative market importance of product functions.
- Calculate the maximum allowable cost for providing each function.
- Continue rolling through these three stages of inquiry at progressively lower levels of the product until arriving at the maximum allowable cost for each critical part.

Of course, this should serve only as a guide, not as an inflexible rule. But it does provide a good place to start when faced with the almost inevitable challenge of taking cost out of the product—without adversely affecting product performance. Northern Telecom (now Nortel Networks) used target costing when designing the Harmony telephone. Having designed the voice transmitter assembly to be installed in the telephone handset, the design team found that the cost of the chosen design was twice the allowable target. Consequently the designers found a much less expensive microphone than that initially chosen, although the performance of the alternative microphone was much more variable than the original. Faced with the challenge, the transmitter design team designed a new manufacturing process for the transmitter that allowed the transmitter to be built at the original target cost, using the lower-quality microphone but maintaining the overall quality and performance of the transmitter as designed. Had target costing not been used, it is likely that the product would have been introduced at considerable loss to Northern Telecom.

Process Design

There is not a great deal to be said about process design that hasn't already been implied; it is important, though, that the design team keep process design and process technologies in mind at all times.

If you have accurately identified market needs and expectations and have accurately translated these market-expressed needs and expectations into words and images that can be understood inside the company, you will have a very clear understanding of the product you should manufacture. If you have done design analysis and creative thinking appropriately, you will have designed the constituent elements of the product from parts up through major systems. Then—and only then—should you finalize the design of the various manufacturing processes and organizations, as well as the control systems that will ensure that the manufacturing system functions effectively.

A detailed discussion of the various aspects of process design is beyond the scope of this book. Suffice it to say that process planning, process fault tree analysis, process FMEA, control charts, and the like are critical to the success of the product, for all the good work that has gone into design will be for naught if the processes are not adequately designed and controlled. If, on the other hand, you design appropriate processes and operate them effectively, what you produce should be what the market wanted. But you cannot satisfy the market if the product is not able to be manufactured in such a way that you satisfy both the market's and your own needs. To that end, you need to ensure that engineering and manufacturing involvement starts early in the design process.

Organizing for Design

The most important aspect of design is organizing for fast response and effective design. There are four basic principles in the detailed design organization for a major product:

1. The organization structure should reflect the build chart for the product.
2. The design executive team should be as small as possible but should have representation from all the critical constituencies, including, where possible, other value chain and customer representation.
3. The organization should be designed for maximum concurrent activity and ease of information flow.
4. Lower levels in the design organization should not be staffed until necessary.

W. Ross Ashby, an early cybernetics engineer, developed an important guiding principle of organization design he called his "law of requisite variety." The law states that control can be maintained only if the variety of the controller is at least as great as the variety of the situation being controlled.[1] In the design organization this can be interpreted as the product project team's reflecting the various constituencies involved in the manufacturing and distribution of the product and also having all the skills and knowledge necessary to identify and resolve issues involving the various modes of use and functions of the product.

> *The fewer the people necessary to provide the requisite variety, the better.*

The issues with which the product project team will be involved are more strategic and operational than they are technical; as lower levels in the product are designed, the nature of the task changes to a more technical role. Figures 11-4 and 11-5 show typical design organization hierarchies, and representative relationships at each level. Figure 11-4 describes the principle of "managing two down."

Effective design means fast response design; the more quickly you can get a product into the marketplace after the market's needs and expectations are known, the smaller the degree of change in those needs and expectations. Needs and expectations tend to change as customers obtain new information. Although you might expect this transformation to be reasonably gradual, quite dramatic changes may occur when competitors introduce new products or market conditions suddenly change. Under these latter conditions it is even more important to be able to quickly put an effective product into the marketplace.

Fast response design does not mean taking shortcuts. To the contrary, organizing for concurrent design activity at different product levels will actually increase the amount of time spent thinking about and designing discrete elements; it is the elapsed time that is shortened. And the elapsed time can be shortened only by making sure the design teams are working with good information, by ensuring that essential coordination occurs, and by demanding that the design process be iterative, not linear. In other words, there is no such thing as "right first time" in design; it is "better each time."

Also given the need to make sure all the necessary skill and knowledge sets are applied where necessary throughout the design process, the number of people working on the product project will probably be greater using concurrent design principles than in traditional "over the wall" design processes. The gains come later in the development process, with fewer people required to perform damage control or modification activities as the manufacturing team tries to bring the new product on line.

Project Leaders

Leader are made, not born, and project leaders have to be developed internally. A great deal has been written about leadership

(text continues on page 192)

Figure 11-4. Typical design organization hierarchy based on the principle of "managing two down."

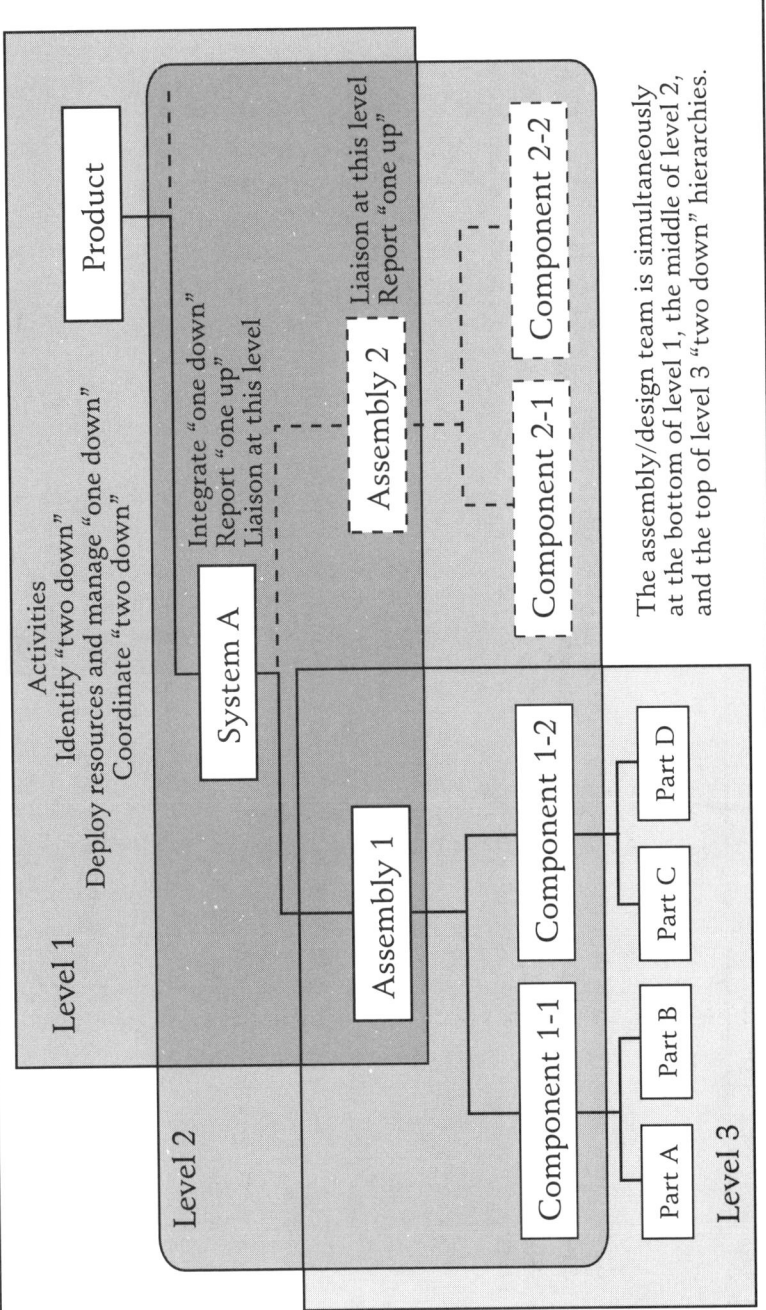

(continues)

Figure 11-4. (Continued)

The Principle of "Managing Two Down"

The principle of managing two down derives from the military practice of field commanders identifying possible tasks for their unit in terms of units "two down" in the hierarchy. A regiment's commanding officer will identify "company-size" tasks, assign task priorities, and then group tasks so that battalions (the unit subordinate to the regiment, but superior to companies) can be deployed. At Division level the general officer commanding will think in terms of battalions, then task brigades or regiments. This principle applies to both offensive and defensive operations.

Thinking in this manner requires the commander to understand the most critical activities facing immediate subordinates and to understand the activities two down that will require coordination, especially across subordinate unit boundaries. Armed with this knowledge, the commander can ensure that the coordination is monitored at higher levels, ensuring an integrated implementation of the plan and a seamless execution of the whole process.

This also requires an effective communication plan to be established at each level in the organization, with deployment being effected "top down," and effective, integrated execution being managed "bottom up." This leaves those closest to the action managing the execution, with those at higher levels managing operational exceptions, while focusing more on strategy setting and deployment.

Commanders "two down" know and understand the critical tasks facing the commander "two up," and hence know what is critical for them to accomplish, and what their role is in the higher-level operation. This deployment procedure cascades down the organization, and coordination and integration "cascades up."

There is no reason this policy cannot operate effectively within manufacturing organizations, or across the new product developmental process.

Figure 11-5. Design hierarchy.

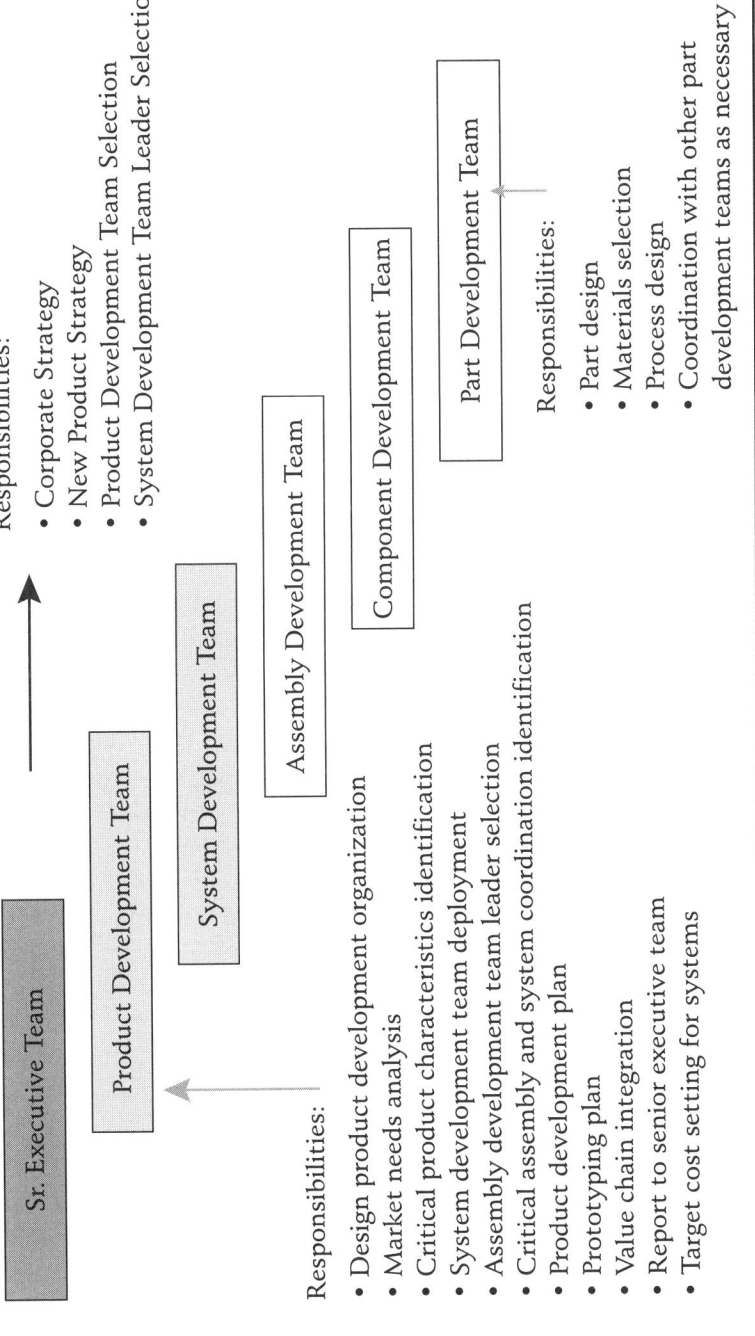

and change management. For our purposes, a good project leader has the following characteristics:

- An interest in the project and the product
- Good interpersonal skills
- Competence in at least one technical aspect of the project
- Good strategic sense
- Good decision-making skills
- Good experience in project management

There are many tests available to identify some of these characteristics; most, however, are developed through experience and guided development by mentors. You are likely to find the next good product development project leader within the ranks of those who have demonstrated their abilities on other projects. What does this statement imply?

1. Among other things, development projects ought to serve as personal development stages for potential project leaders and as evaluation mechanisms for identifying the next new project leader.
2. Companies ideally need to engage in development projects on a continual basis so that project organizational and leadership capabilities can be developed and maintained.
3. Project leaders ought to have some stake in the product to ensure their enthusiasm is maintained at all times.
4. Project leaders should move out of the design organization when the development ends, thus making way for new project leaders.

One way of achieving the latter two points is to appoint the project leader to a position of strategic importance with the new product once the development is complete. One option is to promote the project leader to head the strategic business unit that will manufacture the product; where this is not possible, some subordinate line management position involved with the product after launch is desirable.

Summary

The proactive product development system is not earth-shattering; it is, in fact, quite simple and straightforward. It does require effort and attention to detail, but at all levels it is attention to market-focused and essential detail. Because there is a reason for the effort beyond that of filling in time, people ought to be charged up about the challenge they face. Because the effort is coordinated by personal attention of people at all levels, and because essential information is quickly and personally communicated, the results ought to be seen quickly and the benefits shared by all. And because it is a creative, team-based approach, everybody involved ought to be able to challenge themselves, use their current talents, and help develop or extend their capabilities—all at the same time.

If out of this comes a product that captures market share and improves the company's competitive position—and profitability—the effectiveness of effort is manifest. Who wouldn't want to work for an organization that allowed people to be effective and help make the company effective in the most enduring way—in the marketplace? Moving from hit-and-miss product development to a proactive, planned, and consistently successful approach is a powerful way to empower people to develop powerful products.

Note

1. W. Ross Ashby, *Design for a Brain* (London: Chapman and Hall, 1952).

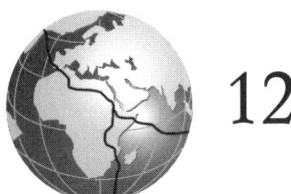

12

Experimentation and Rapid Prototyping

What would happen if every major new product development project you completed incorporated all the functions and elements needed by the customers, the design integrated all the elements effectively and at best cost, and you were able to get the product to the market in half the time it usually took to complete the design process? You would expect to sell a lot of products and to have some very satisfied customers. And you would have some very happy and satisfied people inside the company, particularly in manufacturing. These folks would be happy because the product ramp-up and launch would have been quick, effortless, and with few quality problems. And they would be eager to undertake the challenge again.

In a typical development project in North America, half the elapsed time lies between the official completion of the design phase and the product's market introduction. Why is this so? There are several possible reasons:

- Design changes
- Design corrections
- Process design and engineering
- Machinery and tooling purchase or design and manufacture
- Pilot production
- Workforce training

- Process installation
- Production learning and ramp-up to operating speed

It is a sad fact that a great number of minds and bodies are engaged in pilot production and manufacturing ramp-up figuring out how to overcome design problems. Knowing that there are going to be a number of design changes to the product—and possibly to the manufacturing processes—makes engineers and manufacturing managers reluctant to design and produce tooling and any specialist machinery until the inappropriate designs are resolved.

The impact of this is serious. Costs increase, morale suffers, individual reputations and careers suffer, second-guessing and detail-ignoring occur, product launches are delayed (often for a considerable time)—and the product might not satisfy customers' current needs and expectations!

None of this is necessary. You can eliminate a significant number of problems by designing products to be manufactured. You can get good information about needs and expectations from the appropriate market segment.

Why Experiment?

People and organizations need to experiment to learn, and they need to learn in order to develop or get better. The most critical circumstances in which experimenting for improvement occurs in a company is when it is facing recurring problems linked to critical performance of either a product or a manufacturing process. We also need to experiment to find out what customers cannot tell us about their needs and expectations in a new product. And we definitely need to experiment when we are working with untried or uncertain combinations of technologies.

> *Designing it right requires less time and effort than making it right.*

In essence we need to experiment to better understand something with which we are familiar, or to begin to understand something with which we are presently not familiar. These fundamentally different questions require different approaches to experimenting. So we need to think about how to experiment.

Experimenting and Product Development

The typical experiment associated with product development is a physical experiment, with the focus being on some performance aspect of the product or a component of the product. Test firing of rockets and the use of experiments to test materials are examples of this. In this instance the experimenters are looking for answers that will be able to be reproduced by other researchers, the expectation being that physical properties will be stable. Establishing the experimentation protocols is straightforward, and the technical people can be left to get on with the job.

There is another set of physical experiments that do not lend themselves to either straightforward execution or quick results. These experiments involve people as test subjects working with products or services, with their interactions observed and assessed. Test marketing of products or ideas falls into this category, with the most valuable insight often being about service expectations of customers.

There will be circumstances in which target customers do not know what they want, because they do not have relevant experience. Customers can tell you in detail what they don't like about a product or service; they can tell you reasonably well whether or not the level and type of service is more or less satisfactory. But you cannot solicit from them new service ideas. And you cannot take this one step further and determine the impact that adding services will have on the effectiveness of the overall service. To find these things out you probably have to experiment.

Singapore Airlines has a reputation for a couple of things.

The first is for being the best airline in the world, an honor bestowed annually for many years. That award and reputation are based on service performance in the presence of the customer. The second is for being an organization that experiments. Singapore Airlines has traditionally experimented by making temporary changes to cabin services on specific routes for one- or two-month periods. Examples include having a chef cater freshly prepared hot food in the first class cabin, having a four-member band perform on the upper deck of a 747, and installing slot machines at the rear of the main cabin in a 747.

These experiments were not designed to see if customers appreciated and wanted each of the experimental services. The experiments were designed to see if the concept of the service was appreciated by the customers and to see what, if any, impact the experimental service had on the overall service performance in that particular cabin. For example, the experiment with the slot machines showed that the concept of playing games was popular with a broad range of ages and nationalities. The experiment also showed that the queues to play the machines interfered badly with meal and drink service and with people trying to get to the toilets. The inference was clear: Keep people in their seats while they play games, thus keeping the aisles clear for other service offerings. Armed with this information, Singapore Airlines and its suppliers developed electronic games and other video entertainment for the seats in all cabins, an industry first.

It doesn't seem reasonable that Singapore Airlines continually leads the pack in a high-contact service industry; services are too easily copied (and rapidly copied) for a company to maintain a competitive advantage. Yet Singapore Airlines does it. How? The secret may be simple. By experimenting and by following up with interviews and focus groups, the airline knows why it is making a change to its services and what the overall impact of those changes will be. Copycats quickly identify and replicate the *what*—the tangible aspects of the service. But they don't necessarily understand the *why* and therefore don't understand the impact on overall service performance—and the impact on the customer. Singapore Airlines focuses on value to the customer, and most copycats don't; they focus on cost cutting. Experimenting with novel concepts appears to pay dividends.

There is no reason to suppose this approach shouldn't work with industrial products; in fact, it should be easier given the likelihood of co-opting a willing customer. Singapore Airlines's success shows that experimenting to better understand customers' expectations of how service should be provided is a profitable undertaking. And as the service bundle for the typical manufactured product continues to grow and become more complex, understanding how effectively you are performing on service needs to be tested regularly.

Prototyping

Prototypes are a form of experiment in that the organization is generally testing some aspect of the new product or of the process by which the product will be built. Prototypes also perform other functions that are generally operationally significant but sometimes strategically important. Strategically, a prototype may be the means by which a trial product concept is communicated to senior management, which will decide whether the concept is appropriate for further development for the target market segment. Prototypes are also useful communications devices within the organization and throughout the appropriate value chain; a physical mock-up is worth a thousand pictures (or blueprints). The prototype may also be used by others to evaluate either the product or some aspect of the product's manufacture or postsales service. And a prototyping plan can be a very useful way of establishing and then monitoring the product development schedule. Put more simply, prototypes and the prototyping process are not the prerogative of the designers and

> *Don't forget services when thinking about experimenting.*

engineers; they are the responsibility of the product project team, and they are a key management tool.

Traditionally, prototyping has tended to occur after basic design has been finished and before pilot production is undertaken. Whatever the merits of a single cycle of prototyping, there are at least two fatal flaws in such a process. One major flaw is that in prototype building there will normally be a conflict between satisfying the designer's requirements (faithfulness to the original concept) and satisfying the builder's requirements ("closeness" of the prototype and the pilot production process to the marketed product and the full-scale production process). Handcrafting products that will be produced by semiautomated production satisfies the designer more than it does the manufacturer.

The other flaw is more critical; the organization in general, and executive management in particular, has more ability to influence the product before the final concept is approved. Trying to influence the product design at the pilot production stage is going to be expensive, because much of the design effort will have been wasted. Changes will also result in delays, therefore putting in question the organization's ability to satisfy customer requirements when the product is finally launched. And the impact through the value chain (and inside the organization itself) may seriously harm sensitive relationships.

One way of resolving this is to use prototypes from an early point in the development process. Periodic prototyping is one such development. In this system the prototyping activities follow a predictable path, each stage tied to some significant milestone in the development process. The four cycles are often described as:

1. Physical simulations
2. Computer simulations

> *Early prototyping pays disproportionate dividends.*

3. Mechanical prototypes
4. Production prototypes

Physical simulations (basic models and mock-ups) and computer simulations perform useful functions during the first two cycles. Both physical and computer simulations allow for product assessment by targeted customers and senior management and for concept clarification. They also provide a good basis for cost estimation and for beginning the supplier bid process. The common understanding that a physical representation can generate is unquestioned. Computer simulations, though, take simulation prototyping to new heights by allowing dynamic simulation to show the impact of making changes to the product, with each interested group aware of the impact of particular changes on all interest groups.

Mechanical prototypes of subsystems and components allow the design team to select from competing design concepts, enhance multifunctional design team coordination, and allow the product and its manufacturing processes to be more effectively integrated. One increasingly important role is in testing the subsystem's environmental robustness, with implications for subsystem life and on-line performance.

Production prototypes are full-system models. The most obvious role is testing the buildability of the product and the suitability of the planned production process. But production prototypes can also be useful in helping to drive the product schedule by being obvious reminders of where holdups are taking place in the development process. And production prototypes will always be good predictors of ultimate product quality, whichever dimension of quality is used.

An important consequence of prototyping early is that feedback is received early from those whose input is needed—potential buyers, other members of the supply and distribution

Prototypes help to eliminate confusion and misrepresentation.

chain, and senior management. The better the information you have, the better the knowledge and understanding you have with which to undertake the final design of the product and its attendant services and the more likely you are to satisfy the market segment you have selected. And the cost of developing and modifying simulations is relatively small, so you essentially buy good information and develop good understanding at a low cost. You need to invest more in each prototype the closer you get to full-scale production.

Using periodic, or progressive, prototyping allows for minimizing the risk of wasting money in the development process. The riskiest prototypes are always the first ones, because the company's understanding of what is required is much lower than its understanding of the product when it's time to prepare for pilot production. And the riskiest prototypes are the lowest-cost prototypes, allowing you to test several different prototypes in the first cycle—if you so choose.

These characteristics of early prototypes are impressive. But that doesn't mean you can pay only lip service to later prototype cycles. You are probably aware of the breadboarding phenomenon in electronics development—the use of standard circuit boards on which to place components for a new product or product module. Breadboarding is all about functionality, not fit or lifetime performance. Breadboarding, in fact, deals with only one aspect of the product and provides no insight into how the whole system will work, or even about how easy it will be to manufacture the finished circuit board. The design team, therefore, should accept that it may need to revisit the design once other considerations begin to surface.

Operational Issues in Prototyping

As stated previously, prototyping, or rather the management of the prototyping process, is the responsibility of the product development team. To manage the process effectively, the team must consider at least the following issues:

- What is the dominant orientation of the prototyping process?

- What is the focus of the prototyping process?
- Who controls all or each of the prototyping cycles?
- Who is responsible for building each of the prototypes? Where?
- What is the role and degree of involvement of other value chain players, including customers?
- What are the criteria to be used to assess each test?

- *Dominant Orientation.* Will there be a dominant orientation, as discussed in Chapter 5? If so, will it be technology, market, manufacturing, supply, or distribution, or will it be more integrated and balanced? The relative importance of the engineering, manufacturing, and market considerations will be different in each case. Understanding which orientation is dominant is important, because the product project team will likely be headed by an engineer when technology and supply dominant orientation occurs, a marketing executive when the dominant orientation is either market or distribution, by a manufacturing executive when that dominant orientation exists (a rare but still-observed phenomenon), and by a senior executive with product development experience in the integration-dominant orientation. The projects led by both the engineering and the marketing executives can be readily found in traditional prototyping and product development organizations. The integration dominance is found only in team-based product development and only then in teams that have considerable discretion and contain experienced team members. The dominant orientation will also indicate the mix of skills needed by the project team; superior management and interpersonal skills will be at a higher premium in the integration-dominated prototyping process.
- *Focus.* Will the focus be evaluating the design from an internal, technical perspective; from an external, customer perspective; or from an integrated, management perspective in which all major stakeholders' interests are taken into account? This will influence the type of prototyping conducted and will influence the time over which the prototyping process extends. Focusing purely on design evaluation, for instance, can easily

cause you to ignore issues such as manufacturability and serviceability of the product.

◦ *Control.* Who controls prototyping: engineering, manufacturing, or the project team? Traditionally, engineering has controlled prototyping up through pilot production, with manufacturing getting involved perhaps in pilot production but always in the ramp-up to full-scale production. Given a typical functional organization, the engineering focus will be on the design, not on manufacturability, unless design for manufacturability and assembly (DFMA) principles are used. Even where DFMA principles are applied, however, there is no guarantee that the handoff between engineering and manufacturing will be smooth and effective. Where control of all the prototype cycles is vested in the project team, the transitions between cycles will be more effective. The final product, too, should be more effective when control is vested in the project team; neither engineering nor manufacturing can be expected to be aware of all the interests of all the stakeholders and will therefore ignore anything that is not obvious.

◦ *Building Responsibility.* Who is responsible for building each of the prototypes? This can range from subcontractors, to internal model shops, to manufacturing plants, and even to the production lines themselves. Subcontracting can be valuable if time is a major constraint, but issues of confidentiality and security and a lack of access by the subcontractor to essential internal knowledge will likely limit subcontracting to the early stages of product development. The most appropriate process seems to be to have engineering build the early cycle models, with the responsibility shifting to manufacturing as soon as possible.

◦ *Customer Involvement.* When will customers be involved, and what should you expect of them? When you involve customers only in field testing of final (or near-final) products, the communications process and the customer liaison organization will be small. Contrast that with the decision to involve customers in testing and evaluating prototypes at all stages of the process, including field testing of near-final products. Early involvement of customers will also likely surface design problems that will need to be rectified before subsequent prototyping

> *Involving customers in early prototyping might lengthen the design process—but shorten the overall product development process.*

cycles are conducted, which means that the overall prototyping process will probably take longer when customers are involved early. This time extension is generally expected to be a small price to pay for better information, a better product, and a much greater savings than if a number of design changes had to be made after pilot production or even later.

- *Test Criteria.* What are you trying to achieve at each stage of the prototyping process? Traditionally, early testing focused on product component functionality, with product system functionality being the focus only late in the process. In an integrated process, system functionality will be the focus at all times, with both product and manufacturing process functionality being important. To achieve consistency of focus in the integrated process, the product team should consider developing a testing plan. This plan will include tests appropriate to the product at that stage of its development but will also include tests to assure the product team that the prototype, in critical aspects, sufficiently represents the product that production will build and customers will receive to make the tests both technically useful and effective in communicating information to the manufacturing plants and to critical customers.

Until these issues are resolved, the prototyping plan cannot be fully developed, and the organization supporting the product project team cannot be established. And without the prototyping plan, and the timing of each of the prototyping cycles, the management milestones for the project cannot be established. Because prototyping is such an integral part of the proactive product development system, the completion of each of the cycles becomes a major management milestone.

The prototyping plan must be properly developed and communicated, because other members of the supply and distribution chain should be involved with prototyping as well. (That includes the internal chain; how often do companies focus on marketing issues in product development and ignore sales issues, for example?) The results need to be communicated effectively to the appropriate places at appropriate times. If you are concerned with rapid product development, you need to ensure that you can achieve that and then plan for it. Most companies won't be involved with the scale of prototyping and testing involved in the design of a large passenger aircraft, with experiments and prototype production and testing being conducted all over the world and with the results affecting work in many countries. The communications issues are obvious and need close management. But the difference between most projects and an aircraft development project is really only one of size; the minute you conduct experiments and build and test prototypes across two organizations, the need for effective management of the process increases. If you don't recognize that, or underestimate the effects of an informal approach to cross-organizational communication and integration, the ability to prototype rapidly and effectively will be seriously jeopardized.

Learning

One advantage of a multiple cycle prototyping process is that the amount of learning about the product and its manufacturing process is deliberately limited at each cycle. This ought to make learning more effective and allow for an easier translation of learning into design.

But there is another aspect of learning, too—learning about the prototyping process itself. Managers need to be keenly aware that their contribution will most likely be in the area of organization and coordination, and the prototype development process will always be subject to better organization and coordination. Someone will therefore need to develop tests of prototyping process and organization effectiveness and develop a testing plan. The testing plan will require debriefing the people involved in the process. Better information makes the people in

> *Learning how to learn effectively is a critical competitive competence.*

the process the logical place to start when thinking about improvements.

Changing Behaviors

It doesn't take too long in most large manufacturing companies to discover that manufacturing and engineering organizations resist change. Even in small organizations there appear to be reservations concerning change emanating from engineering and manufacturing. At least, that is what the marketers say, and the evidence appears to support them. New product ideas are received with suspicion, new methods for manufacturing products are rejected or sidelined, and new ways of organizing manufacturing are greeted with any number of reasons why they won't work. But the marketers aren't immune to criticism; maintaining products in the portfolio too long, rejecting market research results, and ignoring manufacturing's problems are often cited by engineers and manufacturers in the firm. These are all serious roadblocks to progress, because they delay and likely reduce the impact of change. If that change is based on clear market segment need, not doing it right creates major strategic and performance problems for the company.

Whether there is good historical reason for such distrust and reactive behaviors is not relevant, nor are the attitudes of the people involved. We are concerned solely with behaviors, because we can observe behaviors and we can modify them. Or,

> *Seems it's always others who resist change, not us!*

if all else fails, we can reassign the people. Let's try to change the behaviors first, however.

○ *Self-Discovery.* The most effective way of modifying behavior is to not have to do it; instead, have the individual discover that his or her behavior is inappropriate and change it. Working in teams can be a powerful catalyst for this, because individual team members have to modify past behaviors anyway to enable the team to be fully effective. Coaching is critical.

○ *Issue or Problem Ownership.* Sometimes behavioral problems are issue-specific; marketers are reluctant to do something about a badly balanced product portfolio, or engineers are not interested in rethinking how to manufacture a particular product. One way of resolving this is to give the individual or the group a larger issue with which to deal, of which the particular problem is one subset. This will force ownership of the problem, which will have to be dealt with effectively as part of the total solution. Invariably the larger issue will require a multifunctional team to be deployed to meet the challenge, and different viewpoints from other than close peers often encourage the unfreezing of behaviors in what is seen as a less threatening environment. The issue should not be an urgent one, because it will take time for the affected people to make the necessary adjustments and accept that change is necessary. The process needs to be well supported, too, because the team has to be encouraged to unearth and present the facts in ways that make it impossible for the target individuals to avoid dealing with the issue.

○ *Changing the Reward System.* Most people act in ways that give them the greatest rewards; change the reward system and the behaviors will be modified. A reward system should do two simple things: It should reward appropriate behavior and penalize inappropriate or deviant behavior. But don't think that the financial rewards at work are the only reward systems available. The social system in the workplace rewards and punishes people at least as effectively as the formal financial reward system, and most people are involved in networks and relationships outside work that have their own reward systems, too. It is pointless doing something about the financial reward system if it has the

> *Formal reward systems are often less significant than the associated informal systems.*

least impact on behavior of all the reward systems operating on the individual. First understand the people, then attempt to make appropriate adjustments to reward systems under your control.

○ *Appraisal and Reinforcement.* Periodic performance interviews should focus on behaviors only; they are the only things managers observe. If some behaviors are inappropriate, they need to be identified as quickly as possible and worked on. The individual should be advised of the specific acts and should acknowledge the acts took place. The interviewer should then state that the behaviors were inappropriate based on specific outcomes of the acts. Then the individual should be asked why the specific acts occurred and should then be invited to come back in a few days with a plan for modifying the behaviors, which should include specific assistance needed to help modify the behavior. The work group should be encouraged to reinforce the appropriate behavior and shun the inappropriate behavior. Seemingly small things, like thank-you notes, messages of encouragement, recognition snacks at breaks, and buttons can be powerful devices for showing what behaviors the social reward system rewards.

○ *Executive Management Involvement.* Nothing, though, is more powerful than having a top executive clearly state his or her expectations. Modifying behavior in specific groups might best be done simply by having the CEO walk into the group and indicate what he or she wants done and why. Often, in fact, what is now regarded in the company as deviant behavior was unconsciously rewarded previously by other CEOs. Pointing out

> *Recognizing appropriate behavior quickly and publicly is a powerful motivator.*

the need for change and issuing the challenge from the top is often sufficient. And don't send someone without power. Nothing is going to happen.

It is the responsibility of the company to try to modify behaviors where they are seen to be inappropriate. If the behaviors can't be modified successfully in the current work environment, move the individual. If that fails, counsel the individual out of the organization. But it is unfair, unethical, and now probably illegal to simply fire a person whose behavior has become inappropriate. And it may be costly to replace the specific knowledge and capabilities that walk out the door.

Summary

Experimentation and rapid prototyping are effective devices for ensuring that you identify early and accurately the needs and expectations of every unit in the supply and distribution chain and, of course, of the target market segment. Prototypes are excellent ways of communicating and receiving feedback. But the prototyping process needs to be managed effectively to gain the best competitive advantage.

Undertaking several prototype cycles allows you to concentrate on a small number of issues at any time; the fewer the number of issues with which to deal, the easier and more quickly the issues will be resolved. The prototyping plan has to clearly state what those objectives are, how they will be tested, and what the outcomes will be. The plan also has to recognize that the objective is to develop a product the market segment wants, designed in a manner that makes it easy to build in the quantities needed. The product project team must at all times keep in mind the ultimate aim and not be tied down watching issues specific to a particular prototype cycle.

Having a good process in place is important, and learning constantly to improve the process is equally important. The process, though, will not operate itself or improve itself; that requires people. You must ensure that the behaviors of the people in the process are appropriate; if they are not, then the behaviors must be modified.

With all these requirements in place—a good prototype development process, appropriate team and support behavior, good communication and integration throughout the supply and distribution chain, and steady attention to understanding and satisfying the target market segment needs and expectations—the chances of developing an appropriate, and therefore an effective, product become almost certain.

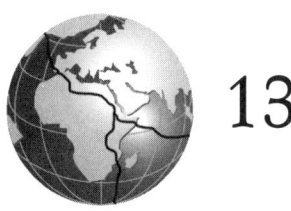

13

From Pilot Production to Product Retirement: Managing the Post-Product Development Process

Wouldn't it be great if you could move a product from pilot production to product launch seamlessly and with minimum disruption? What would happen if you could do that all the time? And what would happen if you were able to meet the target market segment's needs over the life of this new product—and over the life of all your new products? Better yet, what would be the benefits of being able to introduce derivatives or extensions of these breakthrough products at the appropriate time and with the appropriate features for the target customer? The short answer is that you probably wouldn't have much direct competition.

Despite the difficulties associated with the process, many companies do manage to develop the occasional product that succeeds in the marketplace. This success, though, is short-lived when subsequent development founders. This chapter focuses on the process of taking the product from engineering into manufacturing and beyond. The "beyond" includes taking the product into the marketplace and growing the product, and it also includes developing and extending the original product when appropriate. If you do not at least consider the dynamics of the future, success today may sow the seeds for failure tomorrow.

Pilot Production

The focus of pilot production ought to be the validation of the process by which the product will be manufactured and assembled. Many enterprises limit the scope of pilot production to assembly, or even final assembly, although the processes by which parts and higher-level components and assemblies are produced need to be tested and proved before commercial production begins. During the pilot production process, you should be looking to confirm the appropriateness and accuracy of the following:

- Tooling, both automated and manually operated
- Materials handling systems
- Warehousing
- Information and communications systems
- Process layouts
- Work station/work cell layouts, with particular regard to ergonomics

To do this, the pilot production ought to be carried out in the facilities designated for early commercial production. It is the people in the process that make it work or not, and the processes should be designed to allow the people involved to do the job they want to do.

Many large companies carry out their pilot production in specialist engineering facilities, distant from manufacturing plants and the manufacturing reality. Specialist pilot production facilities are job shops, bearing little if any resemblance in any aspect to any manufacturing plant. Without careful managerial oversight, these pilot facilities can confound the pilot production trials by doing any or all of the following:

- Using engineers, not line workers, to build the prototypes
- Using a hand-build or short-run approach to production

- Using tooling other than actual production tooling
- Using nonproduction materials
- Installing tooling in other than the production equipment
- Ignoring all but the physical product–building process

Any one of these acts will lengthen the pilot production process and may create quite a delay if the actual commercial production environment cannot perform as hoped. And delay adds costs and increases the risk of not satisfying target market segment needs and expectations. These practices occur for three basic reasons:

1. The focus of the pilot production is validating product design, not validating the production process.
2. The design process is linear and consecutive, not recursive and concurrent.
3. The designers and engineers do not trust the people in the assembly plants to do a good job, or to have the ability to work through product introduction problems.

The proactive product development process overcomes all of these issues—if the beliefs, value systems, and (most important) behaviors of designers and engineers are consistent with those needed to make the proactive product development system work to best effect. None of these difficulties need occur, and effective management of the process by the product project team ought to ensure that appropriate practices only are observed.

The product project team referred to in the previous paragraph doesn't manage the process; rather, the team integrates the process. The product project team leader manages the process, and managing the transitioning through prototyping cycles is critical. No cycle is more critical than the pilot production prototyping cycle, and the team leader should rarely delegate overall management of this part of the process. Often, this will require the team leader to relocate to the pilot production site for the duration of the cycle. If the pilot production is carried

Teams don't manage; individuals do.

out in the commercial production facility, the team leader should remain on-site until the commercial production is in top gear.

Production Ramp-Up

Ramp-up to full-scale production should be achieved as quickly as possible; the disruption to the commercial production plant should be as brief and benign as possible, for disruption costs both time and money. There are a small number of viable alternatives available:

- Build a new facility in a new location in which to manufacture the new product.
- Close an existing facility and retool.
- Close particular lines and cells and retool/reconfigure.
- Add the new product to the portfolio of products being manufactured using specific processes.
- Stop production of other products and ramp up the new product.
- Add the new product to the portfolio of products, but ramp up the new product while the current products are being produced.

Each approach has merits and proponents, and the product and the anticipated early sales volumes (including pipeline-filling considerations) will be an important factor. Automobile manufacturers generally favor the first two options because of perceived scale requirements. Casio in its watch production practices the last alternative very effectively. The operational issue—which quickly becomes a strategic issue if the operational point is missed—is that production ramp-up is a critical stage of new product development and likely has impacts beyond the new product itself.

Ramp-up can never be considered as an independent activity; it almost inevitably affects other products and processes and always affects upstream suppliers and downstream distribution. If you intend to choose any alternative other than either of the first two, you should ensure that you design your processes ade-

> *Production ramp-up is as critical as any other stage of new product development.*

quately in the first instance. This is a difficult thing to do, and companies generally wind up locking themselves into a design envelope. If this is done knowingly, fine; unfortunately, people don't often understand and acknowledge this, and subsequent product concepts become artificially constrained by what processes are in place.

Identifying the First Production Plant

Whether we conduct the pilot production in a specialized facility or in a manufacturing plant, sooner or later someone is going to have to decide in which plant the first commercial production will be undertaken. This is not a simple decision, except in a company with only one manufacturing plant. The factors to be considered in making the location decision include the following:

- Closeness to the target market segment
- Closeness to critical suppliers
- Closeness to corporate development and engineering organizations
- Overall cost of filling the pipeline and supporting the product launch
- Security and confidentiality
- Past behaviors of plant management
- Plant flexibility
- Process technology fit

Most selection decisions are made solely on the first four of these factors. When the consideration is essentially financial and cost-focused, it is *wrong*. The selection of the plant is strategic and the responsibility of senior management. It cannot be delegated to a subordinate group, no matter how well-intentioned

> *Identifying the most appropriate start-up site is important.*

the group might be, and focusing on financial factors alone is tantamount to delegating the decision to the finance department. There are good strategic reasons for considering the first three factors, however. Also, because rapid learning and adjustment lead to strategic advantage, as a general rule the launch manufacturing plant needs to be located close to the locus of the greatest learning external to the organization.

- *Closeness to Target Market Segment.* In a global industry, there is likely to be a single geographic region that is home to the leading firms in the market segment you have identified as your target. In personal computers it is Taiwan/Korea/Japan, which is one reason that Philips NV's computer monitor group is now located in Taiwan, with early production of each new monitor being carried out in Taiwan, not the United States or Europe. This proximity allows Philips to receive instant feedback from field trials conducted by the computer manufacturers and from minor changes made before the monitors begin being shipped to the largest consumer market—the United States—as part of a personal computer bundle. The short local loop allows for rapid learning, which leads to rapid response.
- *Closeness to Key Suppliers.* Learning and strategic response can be important for and with suppliers as well as key customers. The more critical the operational design elements delegated to suppliers, the more likely key postlaunch learning will involve those suppliers. There are two possible ways of reducing the distance between supplier and manufacturer: locate commercial production in a plant close to the suppliers, or locate the suppliers' facilities and critical people close to the manufacturer's plant. Mitsubishi's aerospace manufacturing division has chosen to locate part of its design and engineering group inside the Bombardier facility in Toronto, Canada, in which the Global Express aircraft is being assembled. This move allows the learn-

ing done during the wing installation on early aircraft to be distributed throughout Mitsubishi quickly and effectively and leads to rapid response through quick design changes.

○ *Closeness to Internal Corporate Specialists.* Support during the ramp-up and launch by corporate development and engineering organizations is likely to be crucial where the pilot production has been undertaken elsewhere, or where the manufacturing organization has been kept out of the design process up to and including pilot production. Full and early involvement of manufacturing people, including line operators, in the design and development process will reduce the need for internal specialists to support the commercial ramp-up. Use of production tooling in pilot production will reduce the need for these same specialists to be present in the plant. The fewer and less significant the potential ramp-up problems, the fewer the necessary specialists. The fewer the specialists (and their support system), the farther away from corporate engineering and design offices the chosen manufacturing plant can be.

Now that the first three factors have been recast in a more strategic learning and knowledge light, away from the financial focus that is generally observed, it is time to think about the other location factors. It should not be a surprise that cost considerations are the least of the concerns, but they are nevertheless real.

○ *Overall Cost of the Launch.* Ideally cost should follow strategy, but financial considerations usually act to constrain the strategy or its implementation in some way. Locating to minimize overall cost is a commonly used criterion and often involves the use of a mathematical model into which estimated costs are injected. Nonquantifiable impacts are generally ignored, or guesstimates of their effect on costs are made by internal experts. As a consequence, the overall cost impact of different potential commercial launch locations is questionable. The results obtained from the mathematical model provide a good point from which senior managers can think about the "real" cost impact of alternative locations; the results should not be used without question, though, and should never be used as the sole basis on which to decide anything, let alone a strategic location decision.

○ *Security and Confidentialtiy.* Where newly developed process technology is to be used for the first time, commercial security and confidentiality are usually important. There is good reason to locate the commercial launch in a plant removed from the chosen target market and away from prying eyes under these conditions. Although the principal market segment may be in the United States, therefore, a manufacturer might decide for security reasons to locate commercial production initially in a Canadian or Mexican plant. Where the risk of failure of the technology is high, in fact, there is often good reason to use the new technology on an existing product in a small and less important market. Technology failure will not have the major strategic consequences in the small market as it would have in the target strategic market with the new product in the public eye.

○ *Past Management Behaviors.* The immediate past behaviors of people are good predictors of immediate future behavior. Managers who have resisted change or who have not supported or encouraged continuous improvement are not likely to provide the critical support the commercial launch requires. Means of changing behaviors are discussed in Chapter 12. Behavioral change takes time to become ingrained, however, and it is probably not a good plan to try to modify inappropriate behavior immediately before commercial launch.

○ *Plant Flexibility.* Probably the most significant factor is the ability of the chosen plant to effectively handle the challenges of a product launch. The product life cycle has significant impact on the market (and vice versa), and therefore on the strategic and operational handling of products over their life. The product life cycle also has significant implications for manufacturing plants. For instance, early in the life of a product uncertainty

> *Flexibility in processes and attitudes is a key issue in start-up plant identification.*

about almost everything connected with the product is at its highest, and uncertainty is at its lowest when the product is in the mature stage of its life. If the chosen plant does not have the manufacturing technology, the organization, and the individual and team training and confidence to handle rapidly fluctuating demand volumes and product mix changes—and minor design changes—the company is courting disaster.

- *Process Technology Fit.* This is possibly the factor that is handled least effectively in plant location decisions, often being sacrificed on the altar of cost reduction. Although the ways in which process incompatibilities can be achieved are almost limitless, the outcomes are usually one or more of the following:

  - Loss of plant focus, with a consequential loss of focus by plant management
  - Lack of skills to manage and operate the new and unfamiliar equipment
  - Inability of maintenance to effectively support the new and unfamiliar equipment
  - Inability of purchasing staff to effectively source unfamiliar materials for the new product
  - Imbalance in the capacities of the various stages of the manufacturing processes, resulting in new and different bottlenecks and new pressures on managers
  - Inability to quickly identify warning signals that indicate problems in overall and specific manufacturing performance

Poor process technology fit results in confusion and cost increases and in serious delays in ramping up and subsequently following demand fluctuations. This can effectively cripple the most well executed product development process.

Consideration of all these factors will help identify the most suitable site for commercial launch. These factors also need to be considered when identifying the second and subsequent plants to manufacture the product. Plant charters might be developed that in fact lead to the development of plant-specific skills that make some plants more effective for product launch than for mature product manufacture, and vice versa. When the sequence of introducing the new product into manufacturing plants is known, the strategy for developing, documenting, and effectively disseminating the newly acquired knowledge throughout the firm can then be determined.

Extending the Product

Successful products are often a prelude for moves to extend the life of the product or for derivatives of the product for different, and often smaller, market segments. As a general rule, any decision to add to the product family, or to extend the market life of the product life cycle, should not be made without the full product development system being used. There are, too, operational issues that product line proliferation in particular brings into play and which must receive the attention of managers before the issues become problems.

Even where parts commonality is possible and practiced, each new addition to the product family increases part numbers, which increases the parts inventory count and value, and almost inevitably increases the amount of finished and unsold product in the distribution chain. Unless this inventory is owned by others, the increase will increase working capital requirements and reduce the strategic cash reserve. When design discipline is lacking and parts proliferate, the working capital requirements become excessive and impede overall productivity and financial performance measures. In addition, the potential for losses due to use of incorrect parts increases dramatically, leading to product quality problems, stockouts of parts and consequent shipping delays, and a demand for more staff to monitor the bewildering complexity created by the combination of product proliferation and the lack of discipline in the whole organization.

The Power and Perils of Platforms

There are two valid and competing definitions of *platform*. One is a new product from which variants are derived over the years.

The Volkswagen Golf (called the Rabbit in the United States and Canada) is an example, from which the Jetta and the Passat were derived. So too is the Boeing 707. The competing form is what is generally called a product family, but which in some industries (particularly the auto and office furniture industries) is called a platform, and which could equally validly be called a system. For convenience, here the single product refers to a platform product, and the system refers to a product platform. Both exhibit much the same promise and potential perils.

Platforms are convenient. It is difficult to design breakthrough products that truly satisfy the target market segment, and in general manufacturers ignore different market segments and more specific needs of subsegments in our target market to focus on the breakthrough. A perfect product or a perfect manufacturing process and organization will never be developed the first time, even for the most effective product; changes will always need to be made to both as a result of the product's being used extensively. It is much easier, though, to make changes based on experience than it is to design the initial product, so refining and incrementally changing an already successful product is generally preferable to developing a new breakthrough product.

Incremental design changes to take the base product into new market segments or to better meet the more specific needs of smaller market segments within the larger initial target market segment can be thought of as filling in the white spaces in the "product market map," and the map analogy is appropriate. The first maps of the globe were generated by people with knowledge of a small portion of the globe (the Mediterranean area or the Middle East) and a vivid imagination. Over time knowledge of the earth's surface has increased, mapping technologies have improved, and communications have improved, so that now there are extremely detailed and accurate maps of every portion of the earth's surface.

Large organizations generally have (or need) more than one platform to cater to the needs of different market segments and to serve different purposes. The sedans, sports utility vehicles, and heavy commercial trucks produced by the automobile manufacturers provide a good example of this. Strategically managing the platform portfolio, therefore, ought to be an ongoing and important function of some senior executive. This is rarely the case in practice, however. All too often the platforms are managed independently of each other, often through the simple and logical device of organizing the company along product lines. One unfortunate consequence of this is a lack of commonality across platforms, particularly for "common" parts such as fasteners and connectors. As every manufacturing manager knows, increasing the number of parts to be made exponentially increases the complexity of the manufacturing task. The real challenge is to reduce the number of parts in total, not to reorganize manufacturing to more effectively handle an overly (and unnecessarily) complicated scheduling and inventory system.

The combination of incremental white space filling and the independence and essential isolation of platform "owners" from each other and the executive management team provides the environment in which the real perils can surface. Customer complaints and suggestions and technology advances become the basis of product improvement; design and engineering biases become the basis for new product functions or uses; marketing biases and customer pressure become the basis for more finely serving particular subsegments of the market; and manufacturing biases ensure that manufacturing processes and organizations do not change. At the same time the platforms begin to overlap, and cannibalization starts to occur. It is time for a major shakeup.

This is admittedly a caricature scenario, and a slightly extreme picture, but it is not an imaginary one. Shakeups need to occur, because in all the biases that play out in the platform development scenario, it is usually the case that the target market segment's changing needs are not addressed. The resistance to change is due to the forces that created the need for change in the first place: internal biases in favor of the self-directed status quo, and the power of ownership.

The feudal system is alive and well in many large companies, and wherever platforms exist a self-appointed liege lord is not far away, often with a personal court in close but rarely observed attendance. In general, the only change welcomed by such a court is one that increases the prestige and power of the

> *Product platforms create the potential for power platforms.*

members of the court; any move to reduce the power and prestige will be fought bitterly and usually skillfully. To avoid a bloodbath it will be necessary to obtain the willing cooperation of the "owner" of the platform and the immediate subordinates, having them accept the challenge of identifying the products that should be culled from the platform portfolio. This requires three things of these managers:

1. That they become conversant with all the company's platforms
2. That they are conversant with the current and projected needs and expectations of the various target market segments
3. That they are or become conversant with activity-based costing and activity-based management

It will not be until the platform managers have a corporate-wide view and the analytical tools necessary to undertake the platform performance analysis that any reasonable results can be expected. And nothing will ever happen if the executive management team cannot understand the recommendations coming from below and do not themselves have the ownership of the overall corporate product strategy.

Platform owners will rightly say that eliminating products will lose the company customers, and that eliminating whole platforms will eliminate whole groups of customers. What is needed, therefore, is a transition to a reduced number of platforms, a transition that follows the following path:

> *Platform strategies are the responsibility of executive management.*

- Development of an overall product strategy
- Identification and confirmation of the target market segments
- Development of new platform concepts to support the new strategy
- Development of the new platforms using the proactive product development system
- Refinement of the platforms to ensure maximum compatibility of parts
- Announcement of timing of withdrawal of current platforms and introduction of new platforms
- Implementation of ramp-up and pipeline-filling plan, and
- Product launch, including dealer and distributor training as necessary

Without a plan for effectively satisfying target market needs and expectations through the transition period—and after the transition—customers will stop buying and move to competitors. Some you may be prepared to lose, but you should accept this solely on the basis of objective strategic analysis and not as a by-product of a flawed product development process.

Summary

If we manage the transitions properly, the long-run future of the company will be assured, all other things being equal. All other things are rarely equal, of course, but even dramatic market or technological change can be accommodated provided the company is appropriately poised to act and decides to move accordingly. Managing the status quo is relatively straightforward, even though in most cases it is complex. Managing the new product development process for a single product is more difficult, especially the handoff to manufacturing for ramp-up and product launch. Even more difficult is managing the transition to product platforms and the management of the ever-changing portfolio of platforms. The most difficult transition to manage is the reduction in the number of platforms and the development of a new base of products from which to undertake the next inevitable round of product proliferation.

The decision to change a product or a platform cannot be effectively implemented without using the proactive product development system in its entirety. In essence this means that the executive management team cannot delegate its responsibility for developing and articulating the corporate product strategy and for insisting that target market segments be identified and their product needs and expectations assessed before any changes take place in any product or any platform. The proactive product development system takes care of the rest.

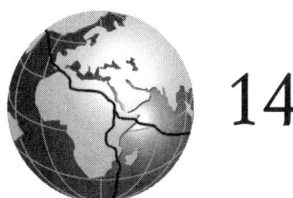

14

Implementing Strategic Product Development

"On the night of October 22, 1707, Admiral Sir Clowdisley Shovell's fleet, returning home victorious from Gibraltar after skirmishes with the French Mediterranean forces, met a disastrous end just twenty miles off the southwest tip of England. Through a fatal misjudging of his ships' position, Shovell wrecked his vessels against the Scilly Isles." The day before, as Dava Sobel writes, Sir Clowdisley had been approached by a member of his flagship's crew "who claimed to have kept his own reckoning of the fleet's location during the whole cloudy passage. Such subversive navigation by an inferior was forbidden in the Royal Navy as the unnamed sailor well knew. However, the danger appeared so enormous by his calculations that he risked his neck to make his concerns known to the officers. Admiral Shovell had the man hanged for mutiny on the spot. The Admiral's refusal to listen led to the death of 2,000 men on the rocks of the Scilly Isles."[1]

Although this sad event had the ultimate effect of precipitating the Longitude Act of 1714 and the consequent search for a chronometer accurate enough for navigation, the story is clearly instructive of the unfortunate consequences of following an erroneous course (no pun intended) despite information to the contrary.

Corporate organizations can suffer from similar attachment to "the way we do it here." Clearly, this book is suggesting a

> "Faced with the choice between changing one's mind and proving that there is no need to do so, almost everybody gets busy on the proof." —John Kenneth Galbraith

new way of "doing it." In this case, it may not be the "admirals" of the corporation who do not listen, but change is always resisted if not handled carefully. It will be important to manage the change and, more important, the transition to the new system over a period of time if the real benefits of these principles are to be realized.

Managing the Transition

The temptation is to make the move to "strategic management of product development" in a series of smaller steps. This is probably a mistake for most companies. As William Bridges points out, "It's not possible to leap a twenty-foot chasm in two ten-foot increments."[2] When you introduce a new product development process as well, it is better and ultimately easier to make the change in one planned but decisive move.

Experience has shown that trying to complete one piece of the triad before embarking on either of the others is to invite the appearance of a "disjointed program" that employees will question, given that they will see only parts rather than the whole. Piecemeal implementation gives time for well-intentioned criticism that may be ill-founded but nevertheless can be

> *Asking an organization to welcome a process like the one proposed in this book is asking employees to welcome change. A certain amount of resistance is to be expected.*

fatal to successful implementation of a strategic product development process.

The Principles of Successful Implementation

There is not enough space here for an exhaustive discussion of all the pitfalls and obstacles you might encounter in the transition to strategic product development. The key principles that usually govern the change, however, are the following:

- Changing to any new approach is fundamentally a people process, not a technical one.
- The executive group both understands and agrees with the chosen direction.
- Implementation is not undertaken with the intention that "we'll see how it goes."
- Someone of sufficient position is responsible for the successful implementation of the program.
- Changes need to be sold to those the change will affect. All involved parties are informed what the direction is, and why. Persuasion is more powerful than edict.
- Specific attention is directed to those who will be directly affected by the changes.
- Education is undertaken at all levels to minimize misunderstandings (and negative reactions).
- Continuous communication is important. Interested parties should not be allowed to wonder how things are going.
- Specific attention needs to be given to unique circumstances that may require modifying the generic approach. Be flexible.

The Churchillian Effect

Winston Churchill is most often remembered for his exemplary leadership as prime minister during World War II. Less commonly known is that he was also a very influential player, at a very young age, during World War I. He was virtually driven from office as First Lord of the Admiralty in 1915 as a direct result of the disastrous Gallipoli campaign.[3] He then spent nearly two decades in a political purgatory between the wars.

In 1914, Churchill, as First Lord of the Admiralty, proposed an innovative and bold plan to strike the Germans where they were most vulnerable and hence break the bogged-down cycle of trench warfare and slaughter under way on the Western Front. The proposal was for a naval effort to force the Bosporus (the natural canal connecting the Black Sea and the Aegean Sea), thus exposing Constantinople, the linchpin to Turkey, to naval bombardment. The plan was ingenious, bold, and timely. The fortresses protecting the narrow straits of the Dardanelles were lightly defended by Turks, with virtually no support from the more formidable Germans in Turkey. What resulted was a debacle of international proportions, which would haunt Churchill for the rest of his life and nearly ended his political career altogether.

What actually unfolded in the operation was the result of indecision, divided counsel, second-guessing, and conflicting orders from beginning to end. What was proposed as a naval operation became an amphibious landing—after fifteen meetings of the war council between November 1914 and March 1915. What was conceived by Churchill as a lightning strike achieving total surprise became the casualty of delay after delay, losing the element of surprise altogether and permitting the Turkish army, aided now by German advisers, to fortify the area well in advance of British attack.

During the extended period of continuous consideration, original staunch supporters of the idea began to have doubts. Some changed positions. Those leading the actual operation demonstrated the same or even greater indecision and timidity shown by those in London. Young Churchill's brilliant stroke to relieve the slaughter in the trenches turned into another front of trench warfare in Turkey. Inept implementation and lack of leadership created a devastating failure. Immediately, the establishment needed a scapegoat, and Churchill was it.

Churchill was right . . . but wrong.

> *A great strategy, if not accompanied by a pragmatic implementation approach, may still fail.*

As discussed earlier, the most brilliant strategy may not be the best approach for every company. Companies have their Gallipolis, too. They don't cost lives, but they cost money, time, and confidence. In the business arena, that is more than sufficient reason to select plans carefully. You must seek the "most appropriate" strategy given the circumstances and resources available.

Know Where You're Going

We've talked about linking the strategic planning efforts of the company to the product development efforts. Likewise, implementing such an important program successfully requires some sort of a road map as well. With any significant program initiative there should be clear expectations of what is required, how much time it will take, and how much it will cost.

Sell the Problem to Be Solved

For some reason people respond more favorably to the need to solve a problem than they do to the chance to exploit an opportunity. Hence, to focus attention you should emphasize the eradication of the negative rather than the securing of the positive.

As Bridges (*Managing Transitions,* 1991) so eloquently points out, "When management and employees recognize the same problem, it puts the manager and the employee on one side, and the problem on the other. By selling the problem, everyone is implicated in the solution."

Focus on the Results Desired

As with any process, particularly one that may be somewhat unfamiliar to those involved, it is all-important to focus always on the end results expected or desired. Make sure everyone knows what a satisfactory outcome is.

In this way, the small glitches will be overcome with a sense of flexibility that becomes commonplace. A rigid adherence to "the rules" is thus avoided in those cases where the published approach needs tweaking. Remember, you want successful products, not mechanical adherence to the process.

Gain Early Results

Take advantage of every opportunity to show positive results from everyone's efforts. Nothing succeeds like success, however small. Long periods of waiting, where there are no visible signs of progress, are very taxing to those involved.

Publish progress and status reports. Share the little victories. Encourage praise for those making unusual contributions. Encouragement, encouragement, encouragement. Stay in touch to ensure that the right things (i.e., the hard-won battles) are the ones praised. Nothing is more transparent than random praise, particularly of achievements the participants know required no particular skill or effort. Know the difference.

Walking and Chewing Gum

Although there is something of a logical sequence to implementing the scheme proposed here, the key is to do several things simultaneously whenever possible. Purposeful, integrated, concurrent activity across the organization is *the* key to rapid new product development and to effective fast response to any strategic or operational challenge, opportunity, or threat. Organization for concurrent rather than consecutive activity is the key to fast and effective response.

> *If everyone knows the desired destination, they can get back on the right road if they find themselves off the track.*

Warts Are Warts

Don't try too hard to cover up the warts. Not everything will go smoothly, and employees know even better than management when things aren't perfect. Acknowledge the glitches and focus on getting it right the next time. To err is human; to ignore the fact is insulting to those who know better. It is entirely possible to remain positive while acknowledging mistakes and correcting the glitches.

Parting Thoughts

It is crucial to stay focused on that which is really important. In every development project there are myriad technical and behavioral considerations that come and go, either dealt with and resolved or simply postponed for later. Minor issues can take on an apparent significance far exceeding their actual importance.

In challenging moments, the right question is generally the most basic: What is the real purpose of this project anyway? When the strategic issues are addressed, and the strategic direction clear, tactical and operational issues become much easier to manage.

Powerful products do not simply happen. They require a powerful development process that depends on timely, relevant understanding of the needs and expectations of strategic market segments and the deployment of an organization capable of effectively exploiting the market understanding. If the knowledge transformation process is well designed, well managed, and founded in the corporate strategy, powerful products will create powerful competitors. And that is the name of the game.

Notes

1. Dava Sobel, *Longitude: The True Story of a Lone Genius Who Solved the Greatest Scientific Problem of His Time* (New York: Walker Publishing, 1995).
2. William Bridges, *Managing Transitions: Making the Most of Change* (Reading, Mass.: Addison Wesley, 1991).
3. Winston S. Churchill, *The World Crisis* (Norwalk, Conn.: Easton Press, 1991).

Appendix I

New Product Decision Screen

Appendix I: New Product Decision Screen

This worksheet is a guide for developing a decision screen for new product opportunities.
Screen development is *not* about "filling out the forms." The purpose of the screen is to provide consistently superior business decisions. Simple, clear statements are always best.

Superior business decisions are the result of the methodical and rigorous processing of decision criteria. Decision screens create these criteria on an infrequent basis (only as often as there is a need for the criteria to change, say, 3–5 years in most businesses) to be applied on a continuing basis. In this way screens can provide for improved and consistently superior decision making.

A well-developed screen benefits the organization in several ways:

- Helps the organization think strategically.
- Encourages synergy within resources.
- Avoids waste of resources by development projects that are a poor "fit" to the capabilities of the company
- Tremendous savings in management time.

Applying the Screen

The screen is intended to be distributed to those in management, marketing, engineering, manufacturing, or design who are involved in developing new products. Simply distributing the screen will serve to improve performance by sharing the criteria for success. If no one knows what the criteria are, the screen will be of little value.

Using the screen will reinforce the process. Violating the screen criteria for "pet projects" will nullify the screen's value as employees see that the rules don't matter.

Managing strategically is nothing more than careful but rigorous planning based on sound information, which is followed by relentless implementation. Decision screens are an important element in making strategic management "look easy."

Appendix I: New Product Decision Screen   239

1. What is the Product?

• A completely new product or line (a discontinuous innovation)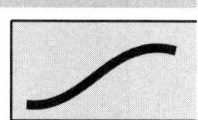

• A line extension or modification of an existing product or line (a continuous innovation)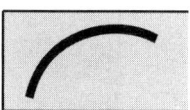

2. The Market Factors:

• What markets (segments) are to be served?

• How is this market currently being served?

• Is the market big enough to be attractive?

• Is the market small enough to be manageable?

• What is the future of the target market?

• What market share is necessary to make this product successful?

• Why will the market accept our offering? Precisely why will *this* product be successful?

3. The Unmet Need

• What is the unmet need satisfied by this product?

• Is there a sustainable competitive advantage? What is it?

4. Strategic Considerations

- Does this product directly support our corporate goals? How?

- Does this opportunity provide us with a sustainable competitive advantage? How?

5. External Influences

- Is this product in concert with economic trends? How?

- Is this product in concert with demographic trends? How?

- Is this product in concert with technological trends? How?

- Is this product in concert with political-legal trends? How?

- Is the product in concert with environmental trends? How?

6. Barriers to the Success of This Product

- Direct competition
- Technology
- Distribution
- Legislation
- Investment requirements
- Skills availability
- Substitutes
- New entrants
- Suppliers

Appendix I: New Product Decision Screen   241

7. Investment Requirements

- Development costs
    Capital:

    Manpower:
- Commercialization-Marketing costs
    Capital:

    Manpower:
- Sales Implementation costs

8. Projected Profitability

• What is the minimum acceptable level of sales or sales growth? Include five-year forecast.

• What is the minimum acceptable profitability on this product or line?

• If premium profits, what is the source of the premium?

• Will this level of profitability continue? For what period? Why?

• What is the return on invested capital?

• How long before desired returns are to be consistently achieved? How long are they expected to continue?

9. Summary Factors

• To what extent does this opportunity satisfy the unmet need?

• What is the confidence level that this opportunity will be successful in meeting all objectives?

• Who is directly responsible for success of this product?

Metal Product Specialties, Inc.
New Product Decision Screen
(EXAMPLE)

1. What Is the Product?

• Clearly describe the opportunity to be evaluated:

Animal-proof architectural chimney cap. This new product (continuous innovation) represents a substantial improvement over existing chimney caps.

2. The Market Factors

• What markets (segments) are to be served?

MUST — The "Conscientious Homeowner" and "Speculative Contractor" segments.

• How is this market currently being served?

• Does the market for this product exceed the 20M minimum? Please specify.

MUST — Overall market potential is estimated to be 23M new construction and an additional 40M in the retrofit market.

• What are the future prospects of the target market?

New construction shows a general increase in the addition of fireplaces.

• Product will meet our third-year minimum share goal of 10%?

SHOULD — Estimated third-year share goal is 15–18%.

• Why will the market accept our offering? Precisely why will this product be successful?

MUST — Proposed product is much more attractive than competitive offerings. Initial estimates indicate lower potential selling price.

3. The Unmet Need

• What is the unmet need satisfied by this product?

SHOULD — Existing products rust out. Proposed product has unique stainless construction.

• Is there a sustainable competitive advantage? What is it?

OUGHT — The design should be patentable.

Appendix II

Strategic Plan Format

STRATEGIC PLAN
FOR THE YEARS
2000–2005

Section I: Mission

Mission statements should define the scope of the business for the purpose of developing for stockholders, management, and employees a common understanding of "why the business exists."

Mission statements should be clear, concise, easy to remember, and used.

Mission statements should focus on verbs: to grow, to satisfy, to produce, to market, to profit, to prosper, to dominate, to lead, etc.

Section II: Values (Optional)

Values define the context in which a business operates. Values are typically defined by the owner(s), board of directors, or chief executive officer. Values state the principles and standards of business conduct that guide the business entity in all of its decisions.

Examples

- The customer comes first, and satisfying customer requirements is the driving force.
- Relationships with customers, employees, distributors, suppliers, and stockholders are conducted in a spirit of partnership that recognizes the need for mutual benefit.
- The company is known for doing what it says it will do. Through its employees, the company keeps the commitments it makes.
- A diverse workforce in terms of nationality, race, creed, color, age, sex, and physical abilities is essential.
- The company and its employees actively support the communities in which they work and live.
- All employees are important contributors and are treated with dignity and respect.

- Integrity is the foundation for all activities.
- Business decisions are made considering the needs of the environment.

SECTION III: BUSINESS SITUATION ANALYSIS

A. MARKET DEFINITION

This section should contain the Market Map(s) visually displaying the total market size by market segment.

If the market map(s) are based on a market segmentation model, then both products and markets can be plotted together on the same map.

If the market map(s) are not based on a market segmentation model, then market size approximation should be based on "product group sales estimate."

"XYZ Industry" Market
Total Potential: $_____Million

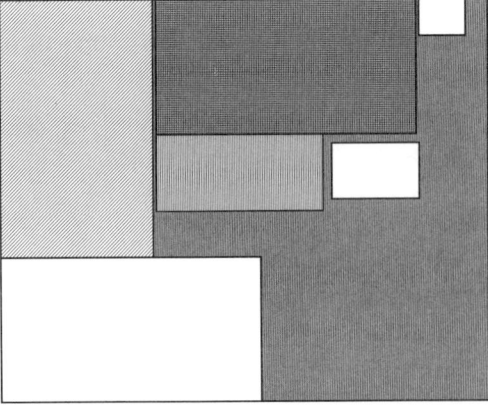

A notation in each section of the market map should indicate the individual market size (in dollars).

A narrative should explain to the reader the significance of the map(s) and conclusions appropriate to understanding strategies contained later in this document.

B. MARKET SHARE

A table listing all segments of all market map(s) with annualized market share should be displayed in this section.

If there is more than one market map, display each market segment together with the rest of the segments that compose the broad product market.

An overall company market share should be calculated based on potential from each map and your annualized sales.

Name	FY XX Annualized Market Share
Industry A	**22%**
Segment 1	19%
Segment 2	23%
Segment 3	12%
Industry B	**12%**
Segment 1	11%
Segment 2	15%
Industry C	**17%**
Segment 1	22%
Segment 2	9%
Segment 3	11%
Segment 4	29%
Total Company	**14%**

C. COMPETITION

The Strategic Group Map(s) should be displayed in this section. Care should be taken to identify as specifically as possible the key factors for success in the industry in which you compete. Once this has been accomplished, this map will display visually how your company and your competitors perform in relation to each other on key factors.

Key Factor 1

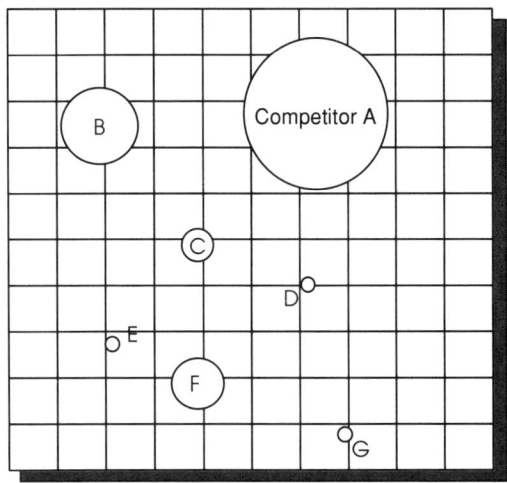

Key Factor 2

Note: Circle size represents the size of each competitor relative to the others.

A table listing all major competitors and their annualized sales should appear next in this section. Estimates of competitor sales can be used but should be noted as such.

Competitor	$$ Volume (000,000s)
A	$ 7.3
B	$ 15.4
C	$ 54.2
D	$ 19.0
E	$125.4
F	$ 31.7

****

The top three to five competitors deserve some further comment. Summary information concerning profitability, strengths and weaknesses, current strategies, probable future goals, and any insight into their management group would be appropriate.

Competitor E

Competitor C

Competitor F

D. PRODUCT

This section should contain both the Product Volume/Profit Matrix and the Product Portfolio Matrix.

The Product Volume/Profit Matrix graphically distinguishes those products that make the highest sales and profit contribution to the business from the rest of the product porfolio. The nine-block matrix is divided into three main categories: (1) higher volume/higher profit products; (2) low volume/high profit to high volume/low profit products; (3) lower volume/lower profit products.

The Product Volume/Profit Matrix

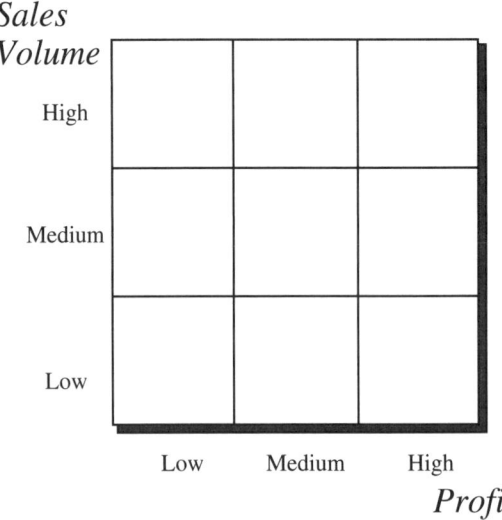

Appendix II: Strategic Plan Format

The Product Portfolio Matrix displays the current product line from a growth rate and market share perspective. This matrix, adapted from the Boston Consulting Group, categorizes products into one of four quadrants. The matrix offers insight into the overall health of a product portfolio from an investment and positive cash flow perspective. It also may indicate new products not yet introduced.

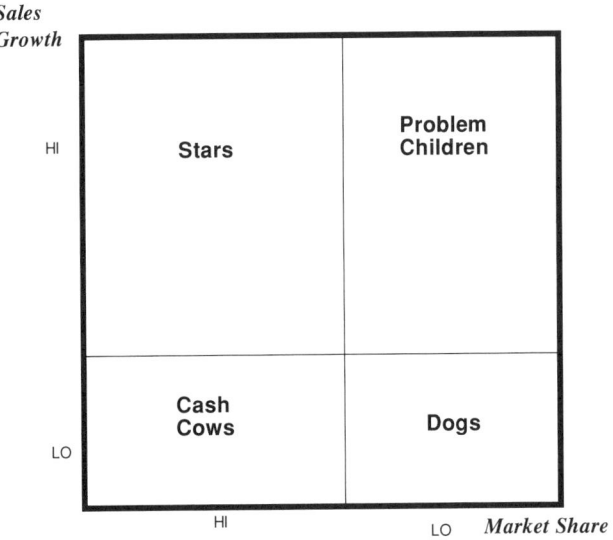

Also included in this section should be the Life Cycle Curve, with your products displayed according to their growth rate:

Development   Not yet introduced

Introduction Rapid sales growth with intensive education and promotion activities

Growth   Growing at an increasing growth rate

Maturity   Growing at a decreasing growth rate

Decline   Sales declining

Appendix II: Strategic Plan Format

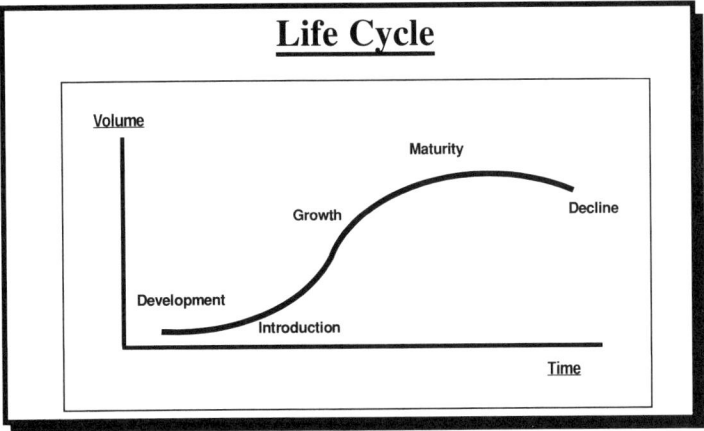

Conclusions should be drawn from these two matrices and the life cycle chart (and other sources of information if appropriate) and listed in a summary section. Based on the conclusions, assumptions for future product management (including new product development) should also be stated.

E. MANAGEMENT ASSESSMENT

A summary of strengths, weaknesses, opportunities, and threats should be listed in this section. Each section should be condensed to no more than one half page in length.

	Capabilities	**Assumptions**
Good	Strengths	Opportunities
Bad	Weaknesses	Threats
	Inside	**Outside**

A separate listing of Core and Distinctive Competencies should be listed with the notation of Distinctive Competencies for those that enable sustainable competitive advantage.

****

The listing of Critical Elements should appear next as the summarized "make or break" items identified by the management team from the analysis of all areas of the business: industry analysis, competitive analysis, capabilities assessment and assumptions, product analysis, customer analysis, and key factors for success.

****

If your business participates in more than one industry, each industry should be displayed on the Life Cycle Curve according to position.

Life Cycle

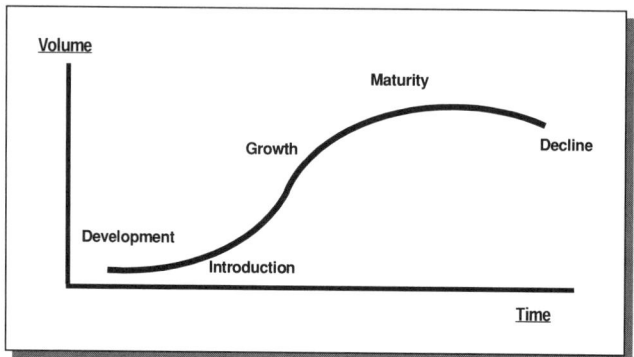

Note: **By this point in the strategic plan, the reader should be able to easily grasp the reason(s) and significance for the following two pages of goals and strategies.**

Section IV: Goals & Strategies

Goals

Goals should be focused on "the result," not "the means."

The statements should be either internal measures (e.g., employee satisfaction, net profit before tax, return on net assets) or external measures (e.g., market share, sales, customer satisfaction).

Goals should not be inconsistent or in conflict with other goals.

Goals should be time-specific and measurable.

Strategies

Strategies should be focused on "the means": the generic strategic directions to be pursued.

Corporate strategies should be brief. This is not the place to provide a long "laundry list" of *tasks* required to achieve goals. Tasks are shown in the annual operating plan.

Several statements in concert with one another should contribute to the specific attainment of the goals of the company.

Strategies may be shared by several functions within an operating unit depending on organizational structure.

Whereas goals are established for a period of 3–5 years or longer, strategies are developed for a period of 1–3 years.

Strategies should:
- Exploit strengths.
- Avoid weaknesses.
- Capitalize on opportunities.
- Employ competencies.
- Use key factors.

The Reality Check

Strategy → BCA Reality-Check Valve → Goal

Strategy utilizes two or more strengths, competencies, or key factors for success.

Strategies do not conform to company strengths, industry opportunities, core or distinctive competencies, etc., but decide to proceed anyway.

Bypass

Section V: Product Sales Forecast Plan

A listing of individual products (by product category if appropriate) along with sales forecasts for each of the next 5 years and for 7 and 10 years should be placed here in table format.

New products in development but not yet introduced should be listed with introduction dates and sales forecasts.

A total by product category and for the entire portfolio can then be used to perform a gap analysis to determine new product/new business development needs for the future.

Sales Forecast (000,000s)

Product	2000	2001	2002	2003	2004	2005
Group A						
Product 1						
Product 2						
Product 3						
Group B						
Product 4						
Product 5						
Product 6						
Group C						
Product 7						
Product 8						
Product 9						
FORECAST TOTAL						

Gap Analysis (000,000s)

Product	1995	1996	1997	1998	1999	2004
Sales goal						
− Sales Forecast						
= SALES GAP						

Section VI: Financial Summary

Page 14 should contain the last 5-year or 10-year financial performance.

Page 15 should contain the financial pro-forma for the planning period associated with this plan document (5 years or 10 years).

Bibliography

Ashby, W. Ross. *Design for a Brain.* London: Chapman and Hall, 1952.

Bacon, Frank R., Jr., and Thomas W. Butler, Jr. *Achieving Planned Innovation.* New York: The Free Press, 1998.

Boothroyd, Geoffrey, Peter Dewhurst, and Winston Knight. *Product Design for Manufacture and Assembly.* New York: Marcel Dekker, Inc., 1994.

Bossert, James L. *Quality Function Deployment: A Practitioner's Approach.* Milwaukee: ASQC Quality Press, 1991.

Bowen, H. Kent, Kim B. Clark, Charles A. Holloway, and Steven C. Wheelwright. *The Perpetual Enterprise Machine.* New York: Oxford University Press, 1994.

Bridges, William. *Managing Transitions: Making the Most of Change.* Reading, Mass.: Addison Wesley, 1991.

Churchill, Winston S. *The World Crisis.* Norwalk, Conn.: Easton Press, 1991.

Clark, Kim B., and Takahiro Fujimoto. *Product Development Performance.* Boston: Harvard Business School Press, 1991.

Clark, Kim B., and Steven C. Wheelwright. *Managing New Product and Process Development: Text and Cases.* New York: The Free Press, 1993.

Clemmer, Jim. *Firing on All Cylinders.* Toronto: Macmillan of Canada, 1991.

Crosby, Philip B. *Completeness: Quality for the 21st Century.* New York: Plume, 1992.

Evans, James R., and William M. Lindsay. *The Management and Control of Quality (3rd edition).* Minneapolis/St. Paul: West Publishing Company, 1996.

Goh, Swee C. "Toward a Learning Organization: The Strategic Building Blocks." *SAM Advanced Management Journal.* Spring 1998, pp. 15–22.

Harrigan, Katheryn R. *Managing Maturing Businesses.* Lexington, Mass.: Lexington Books, 1988.

King, Bob. *Better Designs in Half the Time.* Dearborn, Mich.: GOAL/QPC, 1989.

Law, Bernard, Viscount Montgomery of Alemain. *The Memoirs of Field-Marshall the Viscount Montgomery of Alemain K. G.* London: Collins St. James Place, 1957.

Leonard-Barton, Dorothy. *Wellsprings of Knowledge: Building and Sustaining the Sources of Innovation.* Boston: Harvard Business School Press, 1995.

Meyer, Marc H., and Alvin P. Lehnerd. *The Power of Product Platforms.* New York: The Free Press, 1997.

Michaelson, Gerald A. *Winning the Marketing War.* Knoxville, Tenn.: Pressmark International, 1995.

———. *Sun Tzu—The Art of War for Managers.* Knoxville, Tenn.: Pressmark International, 1998.

Nonaka, Ikujiro, and Hirotaka Takeuchi. *The Knowledge-Creating Company.* Oxford, England: Oxford University Press, 1995.

Noori, Hamid, and Russell Radford. *Production and Operations Management: Total Quality and Responsiveness.* New York: McGraw-Hill, 1995.

Owen, Charles. "Structured Planning: The Computer-Supported Process for the Development of Design Concepts" (Parts I and II). *Design Processes Newsletter,* vol. 2, no. 1, pp. 1–5, and vol. 2, no. 2, pp. 1–5. Design Processes Laboratory, Institute of Design, Illinois Institute of Technology.

Patterson, Marvin L. *Accelerating Innovation: Improving the Process of Product Development.* New York: Van Nostrand Reinhold, 1993.

Pine, Joseph B. II. *Mass Customization: The New Frontier in Business Competition.* Boston: Harvard Business School Press, 1993.

Porter, Michael. "What Is Strategy?" *Harvard Business Review,* January-February 1996, pp. 61.

Sabbagh, Karl. *Twenty-First Century Jet.* New York: Scribner, 1996.

Schilling, Melissa A., and Charles W.L. Hill. "Managing the New Product Development Process: Strategic Imperatives." *Academy of Management Review,* 1998, Volume 12, Number 3, pp. 67–81.

Sobel, Dava. *Longitude: The True Story of a Lone Genius Who Solved the Greatest Scientific Problem of His Time.* New York: Walker Publishing, 1995.

Taguchi, G., and D. Clausing. "Robust Quality." *Harvard Business Review*, January-February 1990, pp. 65–75.

Tanaka, Masayasu. "Cost Planning and Control Systems in the Design Phase of a New Product," in Mondon, Y., and M. Sakurai (eds.). *Japanese Management Accounting.* Cambridge, Mass.: Productivity Press, 1989, pp. 49–71.

Ulrich, Karl T., and Steven D. Eppinger. *Product Design and Development.* New York: McGraw-Hill, Inc., 1995.

Wheelwright, Steven C., and Kim B. Clark. *Revolutionizing Product Development.* New York: The Free Press, 1992, pp. 312–323.

Wilson, Paul F., Larry D. Dell, and Gaylord F. Anderson. *Root Cause Analysis: A Tool for Total Quality Management.* Milwaukee: ASQC Quality Press, 1993.

Index

acquisition, 35
action orientation, 149
Acura, 161–162
adaptive skill, 149
ad hoc team, 100
Adizes, Ichak, 72–74
aesthetics, 155
alterations, of current products, 114–115
ancillary services, 37
Apple Computer, 73
Ashby, W. Ross, 187
assembly, design for, 184–185, 204
audience, 27
automation, 185
automobiles, 161–162, 216, 223
availability requirements, 27

behavior
  change-resistant, 208–210
  of plant management, 217, 220
  and platform strategy, 224–225
  purchasing, 53, 54–55, 58–59
beta testing, 155, 163
Boeing, 223
Boston Consulting Group, 251
breadboarding, 202
Bridges, William, 230
building block approach, 160
bureaucracy, 82

business definition, 36
business to business market, 56–58
buying decision, 53

capacity, 183
career path, 192
Casio, 216
change
  and corporate culture, 78–79
  implementation principles, 231–232
  manufacturing and engineering, 207–219
  and product life cycle, 74
Clark, Kim B., 160
coaching, 208
cold calls, 44
commercial success, 6–7
communication
  and change, 231, 234
  of ideas, 171
  and pilot production, 214
  and prototyping, 199, 201–202, 204–206
competencies
  core *versus* distinctive, 130–131
  developing, 159–161
  management, 254–255
  and opportunity analysis, 140, 143, 145, 150
  see also core competencies; skills

competition
    and decision screen, 89, 94
    differentiation from, 2, 37
    internal, 13–14
    at operational level, 12–13
    and product definition, 37
    at strategic level, 8–11, 14–16, 34–36, 248–249
    at tactical level, 11–12, 44–45
competitive advantage, 143, 239, 242
competitive environment, 142–143, 144, 184–185
competitive imperative, 79–80
competitive products, 154, 168, 171
competitors, 143, 248–249
complacency, 82
components, 180, 205
computer simulations, 201
concept design, 155, 168, 171–172
    and requirements analysis, 172–173
concept investigation, 154
conferencing, see interactive experience group conferencing
confidentiality, 217, 220
construct envelope, 172–175
consumer products, 53, 56
control charts, 186
core competencies, 89, 93–94, 130–131
corporate capabilities, 149–150
corporate culture
    and change, 78–79
    competitive imperative, 79–80
    healthy and unhealthy, 83
    history, 80
    life cycle, 72–74
    management characteristics, 80–81
    mature organizations, 74
    and opportunity analysis, 146–149
    orientation, 74–77
    personality types, 81–83
    and product development, 69–71
    in regulated industries, 80
    values, 78–79, 131
cost
    estimating, 201
    as focus, 2, 61
    of launch, 219–220
    of parts inventory, 222
    and platform strategy, 120
    procurement input, 103
    of product, 172, 185–186
    of prototypes, 202
costing, activity based, 225
critical elements, 255
current products
    analysis, 114–115
    and concept design, 171
    ramp-up impact, 216, 226
    technological impact, 181
    transitioning customers from, 121–122
customer relationship, 44, 66, 107
customers
    analysis of current, 111–114
    involvement of, 106–107, 165, 168, 173–177
    market segmentation of, 63, 64–66, 90–91
    and prototypes, 164, 204–205
    transitioning from older product, 121–122
    and value source, 136–138

dealers, 54–55, 62–63
debriefing, 206–207
decisions
    on future-oriented features, 184–185
    on plant selection, 217–222
    purchasing, 53, 54–55, 181–182
decision screen
    benefits, 39, 89–90, 238
    example, 242
    and product deletion, 115
    revision frequency, 238
    worksheet, 239–241
declining markets, 49
delays
    causes and impact, 195–196
    in pilot production, 214–215
    in prototyping, 200
    see also timing

Index

demographics, 61, 240
design
  detailed, 168–170
  fast response, 188
  last minute changes, 195–196
  for maintenance, 184
  major steps, 153–156
  for manufacturability, 184–185, 204
  versus manufacture, 180
  organizing for, 187–188, 189
  and pilot production, 214–215
  and platform approach, 223
  problems, 155–158, 195–196
  process analysis, 180
design brief, 171–175
design concept, 155, 168, 171–172
DFMA, 184–185, 204
differentiation, 2, 37
discounting, *see* pricing
distinctive competence, 131
distribution chain, 37, 222
distribution channels
  and design and development, 155
  and marketing participation, 103
  and market leaders, 44
  and opportunity analysis, 150
  and platform change, 226
  and production location, 217
  and ramp-up, 216
distributors, 106, 168, 226
domestic markets, 138–140, 142–143
durability requirements, 27

economics
  in decision screen, 91–93, 240
  of product sale, 140
  of product usage, 27
economic value added (EVA), 91, 128
economist culture, 82
employee pride, 131
engineering department
  and change, 207
  input, 102–103, 108, 168, 204
entrepreneurial companies, 81–82
environmental robustness, 201
environmental scanning, 154

environmental trends, 240
equipment
  capacity utilization, 183
  for pilot production, 215
  as resource requirement, 150, 154
ergonomics, 214
executive level
  and change, 231
  communicating with, 199–200
  and concept design, 168
  decision activity, 23, 73–74
  and needs analysis, 154
  and opportunity identification, 125–126
  and production plant, 217
  role, 33–34, 36–39, 88–89, 158–159
  and staffing decisions, 101–102
experience
  and corporate fit, 150
  learning from, 159–160, 206–207
experimentation, 162–163, 196–199
exports, 40–42

facilitating products, 37
facilitating services, 37
facilities
  and corporate fit, 150
  for pilot production, 214
  for production, 217–222
  for ramp-up, 216
  work station layouts, 214
fault tree analysis, 186
features, 120
feedback, 155
field intelligence, 154
financial requirement, 150, 154
financial summary, 260
financing, *see* funding
fishing analogy, 20–21
fishing rod example, 58–59
fit, 183
flexibility
  in change implementation, 231, 234
  of production plant, 217, 220–221
FMEA, 186
focus groups, 163, 198

268 Index

forecasts, 259
functionality
  of components, 180, 205
  in concept design, 170
  and needs analysis, 177–179
funding
  and corporate fit, 82, 150
  executive role, 38–39, 154
  and opportunity analysis, 132, 241
  and success criteria, 90
future features, 182, 184–185
future products, 182

gap analysis, 259–260
General Motors, 161–162
global markets, 39–41
  and opportunity analysis, 138–140, 142–143
  and production location, 218
  segmentation techniques, 57–58
goals, 90, 128, 168, 257–258
golf analogy, 9
growth phase
  of companies, 73, 79–80
  of markets, 48–49
  of product lines, 116

Harrigan, K. R., 49
Heskett, James L., 79, 83
Honda, 172
human element, 157–158, 171

ideas
  ability to express, 171
  for new products, 19–20, 31, 126–127
  see also spontaneous opportunities
image, 132–133, 150
imitators, 45–47
implementation
  of change, 231–232, 234
  of strategic approach, 229–235
industrial products, 31, 53, 56
infighting, 13–14
information
  for current customer analysis, 113

  for design and development, 153–154
  for executive level, 23–25, 26
  for market segmentation, 61, 64, 154
  for operations level, 25–29
  questions, 21–23
  for tactical level, 29–30
  team impact, 158
  for technology, 154
  timeliness, 158, 163
  see also learning; market segmentation
information systems, 214
infrastructure, 182
installers, 106–107
interaction
  between product and service, 183
  between product characteristics, 177–179
interactive experience group conferencing, 57–58, 62–65
interviews, 198
inventory, 120, 222
investment, see funding

knowledge, see information; skills
Kotter, John P., 79, 83

launch
  in proactive system, 170
  and production location, 219–220
  and ramp-up, 155
  and team leader, 192
leaders
  market, 43–44
  of project team, 157, 188–192, 215–216
  style of, 80–81, 83, 88
learning
  from platform, 223
  production, 217–219
  from projects, 159–160
  prototyping, 206–207, 210
legal trends, 240

Index

life cycle
  corporate, 72–74
  multiple industries, 255
  in portfolio analysis, 252
  product, 74, 220–221, 222, 253
line management, 102
location, 217–222

maintenance, design for, 184
management
  activity-based, 225
  characteristics, 80–81, 83, 254–255
  line, 102
  and opportunity analysis, 140
  of pilot production, 214–216
  of platform portfolio, 223–227
  of proactive approach, 160
  of prototyping, 206–207
  of transitions, 226–227, 230–235
  "two down," 189–191
  see also executive level
"managing two down," 189–191
manufacturability, 115, 184–185, 204
manufacturing operation
  and change, 207–210
  efficiency, 116, 120
  pilot production, 155, 200
  in proactive approach, 168–170
  process technology, 154
  and prototypes, 203–204
  ramp-up, 155, 216–217
  streamlining, 224
manufacturing process, 180
Maps
  Market, 246–247
  Strategic Group, 248
margin
  and decision screen, 89, 91
  and needs analysis, 27–29
  as success factor, 6–7
market conditions, 48–49, 240
market factors, 239, 242
marketing department
  focus groups, 163
  input timing, 103
  product launch, 155

market leaders, 43–44
Market Maps, 246–247
market research
  concept investigation, 154
  and experimentation, 197–198
  and needs analysis, 29–31, 173
market segmentation
  for business to business, 56–58
  and current products, 114–115
  and customers, 111–113
  four dimensions, 61, 64
  information for, 61, 64, 154
  model, 24–25, 61–67, 246–247
  role of, 14–16, 19–21, 31, 168
  sales input, 63
  see also target market
market share, 44, 128, 168, 247
materials
  alternative, 103
  in pilot production, 214, 215
  sourcing, 155
matrix organization, 98–99
mature markets, 49
mature organizations, 74
McCarthy, E. J., 35
mechanical prototypes, 201
mentoring, 39
"me too" products, 45–47, 61
milestones, 205
mission creep, 88
mission statement, 95, 127–128, 245
Mitsubishi, 218–219
monitoring, *see* environmental scanning
Montgomery, Field Marshal B. L., 100–101
morale, 157, 196

needs analysis, 51–56
  business to business, 56
  functional needs, 61
  information, 25–29
  and opportunities, 136, 137
  in proactive product planning system, 173–177

needs analysis (*continued*)
  and product characteristics, 174–176
  as product development stage, 154
  and purchasing decision-makers, 53, 54–55
  and surveys, 53–54, 56
  understanding customer, 51–56
  unmet needs, 27, 239, 241, 242
  see also requirements analysis
negotiable conditions, 91
nichers, 47–48
Nortel Networks, 185–186

obsolescence, 181
office furniture example, 54–55
operations personnel, 103–104, 108
opportunities
  analysis steps, 151
  and corporate capabilities, 149–150
  and corporate fit, 130–133
  domestic markets, 138–140, 142–143
  initial scope, 129–130
  qualitative aspects, 140
  quantitative aspects, 138–140, 141
  selection procedures, 125–126
  spontaneous, 133–134
  and strategic plan, 127, 148
  and target market segment, 131
  understanding the opportunity, 135–140
  value source, 136–138
organizational culture, *see* corporate culture
organizational impact
  of new technology, 183
  on purchasing companies, 181–182
organization structure, 187
orientation
  corporate, 74–77
  of project team, 203
ownership, of issue, 208

parts
  functionality, 105
  inventory issues, 120, 222
  in platform approach, 115, 120, 224
  in process design, 180
  recycling, 184
patent protection, 44
performance, 172, 182
performance levels, 120
performance orientation, 82–83
periodic prototyping, 200–201
personality types
  corporate, 81–83
  in project team, 101, 105
personnel
  group conference, 62–63
  manufacturing, 103–104, 108
  marketing, 103, 241
  and opportunity analysis, 140, 150, 241
  organization types, 97–100
  of pilot production, 214–215
  procurement, 103
  of project team, 38, 62–63, 88, 90
  requirements, 90, 100–102, 241
  technical, 102–103
Philips NV, 218
pilot production, 214–216
  control of, 204
  purpose, 155
  timing, 200
planning
  process, 186
  product mix, 122
  for prototyping, 205–206
  versus strategy, 34, 142
  see also proactive product planning
platform strategy
  advantages, 120, 223
  definitions, 118–120, 222–223
  management, 223–225
  and manufacturability, 115
  parts impact, 115, 120, 224
  and product mix, 122
  streamlining, 225–226
  and technology, 182
political trends, 240

Index

portfolio
  analysis, 251–252
  platform, 223–227
positive approach, 234, 235
praise, 234
pricing
  discounting, 45
  as focus, 61
  of future-oriented features, 184
  marketing input, 103
  target costing, 185–186
  and target marketing, 8, 12
prioritization, 126, 155–156, 176–177
proactive product planning
  concept design stage, 168
  development team, 164–165
  executive involvement, 158–159
  experimentation, 62–163
  key propositions, 167–168
  learning from experience, 159–161
  overview, 168–170
  rapid prototyping, 164
  speed to market, 161–162
problem solving, 149, 208, 233
process design, 180
process layouts, 214
process ownership, 157–158
process planning, 186
process technology, 183–184
procurement, 103, 181–182
product construct envelope, 172–173
product criteria creep, 88
product development
  and corporate culture, 69–71
  critical elements, 3, 16
  executive decisions, 23
  major steps, 153–156
  and needs analysis, 154
  organization of, 97–100
  overview, 15
  small and major changes, 163
  strategic activities, 36–39
  typical approach, 85–89
  and value chain, 37
product family, *see* platform strategy
production plant, 217–222

production prototypes, 201
product lines
  analysis of, 116–118
  complex situation, 160
  restructuring, 121–122
product management system, 118
product mix, 120–122, 181
product plan, 122
product planning system, 158–159
products
  characteristics, 174–178, 182, 184–185
  comparisons, 171
  competitive, 154, 168, 171
  core and facilitating, 37
  cost, 172
  definition, 37, 242
  deletion, 113, 115, 159, 226–227
  describing, 171–172
  discontinuation, 113, 115, 159, 226–227
  future-oriented, 182, 184–185
  impact on company, 159, 165
  industrial, 31, 53, 56
  life cycle, 74, 220–221, 222, 253
  requirements analysis, 172–173
  see also current products
product technology, 181–183
Product Volume/Profit Matrix, 250
profitability
  and decision screen, 91–93, 241
  and facilitating services, 37
  as goal, 126
  and platform strategy, 120
  of product line, 116
  see also margin; Product Volume/Profit Matrix
project team
  composition, 187
  concurrent activities, 188
  departmental input, 57, 62–63, 98–99, 102–104
  dominant orientation, 203
  executive mandate, 33–34
  goals, 90
  leaders, 157, 188–192, 215–216

project team (*continued*)
  location, 164–165
  multidisciplinary skills, 102–104
  needs analysis, 27, 29–31
  outside contributors, 106–107
  overview, 15
  and pilot production, 215–216
  and prototypes, 203–204
  size, 104–105
  staffing, 38, 62–63, 88, 90
  and structured process, 105–106
  variants, 99–100
promotion
  and marketing participation, 103
  and opportunity analysis, 150
  at tactical level, 12, 31, 44
prototyping
  advantages, 155, 171
  and communication, 199, 201–202, 204–206
  control of prototypes, 204
  and customers, 204–205
  and delays, 200
  focus, 203–204
  and milestones, 205
  multiple cycle, 200–201, 206–207, 210
  operational issues, 202–206
  orientation, 203
  plan for, 205–206
  responsibility for, 204
  sales input, 206
  and senior management, 199
  for technology, 182, 184
  test criteria, 205
  timing, 200, 201–202
purchasing behavior, 53, 54–55, 58–59, 181–182

ramp-up, 155, 216–217, 226
rapid product development, 206
reality check, 258
recycling, 184
reengineering, 114–116
regulated industries, 80
  see also legal trends

regulatory constraints, 154
repair personnel, 106–107
reputation, 132–133
requirements analysis, 172–173
  see also needs analysis
resources, 154
  see also funding
responsibilities
  in design hierarchy, 191
  for effecting change, 231
  for overall success, 241
  for prototyping, 204
  for sales, 11–12
retail display, 177
return on equity, 128
reward systems, 157, 159, 160–161, 208–209
risk, 202, 220, 224
rules, adherence to, 234

sales department
  market segmentation, 63
  and prototyping, 206
  tactics, 11–12, 44, 231, 233
  volume, 6–7, 89, 92–93, 121–122
sales forecasts, 259
Saturn example, 161–162
security, 217, 220
self-directed team, 99–100
service requirements, 27, 170, 182–183, 184
services, facilitating, 37
shareholder value, 128
shelf life, 177
Singapore Airlines, 197–199
skills
  in decision screen, 240
  for development, 90, 160, 192
  for new technology, 183
  problem solving, 149
  for production, 219, 221–222
Sobel, Dava, 229
specialists, *see* skills
specialization, 47–49, 74–77
speed to market, 161–162
spontaneous opportunities, 133–134

Index

stockpiling, 156
strategic fit, 140–146, 240
strategic focus, 142, 149, 233–234, 235
Strategic Group Maps, 248
strategic plan, 39–40, 110, 126, 127–133
   worksheet, 245–260
strategies
   for attack, 44–45, 46
   for competing, 8–11, 14–16, 34–36, 143–146
   of competitors, 143
   defensive, 43–44
   follower, 45–47
   guerrilla, 47–49
   for large/small companies, 160
   and market conditions, 48–49
   for product mix transition, 122
   in strategic plan, 258
strategy
   computer simulation, 163
   corporate, 128–129, 163
   key principles, 143–146, 147
   versus planning, 34, 140–142
   and platform approach, 226
   in proactive planning, 168
   for series of product lines, 160
   weapons of, 35, 142
strengths, 84, 89, 93–94, 254
subassemblies, 120
subcontracting, 204
subsystems, 201
success
   and attack strategy, 45
   barrier analysis, 240
   and capabilities, 90
   and corporate culture, 80–81, 82–83
   defining, 3–4, 6–7, 39
   key factors, 248
   leadership factor, 88
   and proposal purveyors, 126
   and sales volume, 92–93, 250
suppliers
   bids from, 201
   in decision screen, 240

location issues, 217, 218–219
   and value, 138
surveys, 53–54, 56, 113
system functionality, 205

target costing, 185–186
target market
   customers outside of, 8, 111–114
   in decision screen, 90–91, 242
   description, 38
   expectations, 154
   importance, 8–11, 67
   and opportunity analysis, 131
   and pricing, 8, 12
   and production plant, 217, 218
teamwork, 157–158
   see also project team
technical input, 102–103
technical requirements, 27
technocrats, 82
technology
   acquisition, 154
   buyer viewpoint, 181–182
   and corporate culture, 82
   in decision screen, 89
   and design team location, 165
   new, 132
   obsolescence, 181
   and opportunity, 150
   and platform, 182
   process, 154, 183–184, 217, 221
   product, 154, 181–183
   risk management, 220
   and technical input, 102
   trend analysis, 240
telephone handset, 185–186
testing, 162–163, 205–207
test marketing, 197
timing
   Churchill example, 232–233
   concurrent activity, 188
   of marketing input, 103
   of pilot production, 200
   of platform changes, 226
   of prototyping, 200, 201–202
   of ramp-up, 216–217, 226
   speed to market, 161–162, 188, 195–196

timing (*continued*)
   of transitions, 230–232, 234
   see also delays
tooling, 154, 214, 215, 216, 219
training, 120, 131, 226
transitions
   in product mix, 120–122
   of product platforms, 226–227
   to strategic approach, 232–235
trend analysis, 184, 240
trial-and-error approach, 29
"two down management," 189–191

use modes, 177–179
utilization, of capacity, 183

value, source of, 136–138
value chain, 37, 138, 139
values, corporate, 78–79, 131, 245–246
variety, law of requisite, 187
visibility continuum, 79
Volkswagen, 223
volume, 89, 92–93, 183, 250
   see also sales department

warehousing, 214
warranties, 27, 113
watches, 216
weaknesses, 84, 89, 93–94, 254
Wheelright, Steven C., 160
work stations, 214